Ralph Ottey - Author

CW01020576

and many thanks for your support.
Ralph
20/10/15

Ralph Ottey

Author

Ralph Ottey was just 19 years old when he sailed from his homeland, Jamaica, bound for England to join the RAF and play his part in the Second World War. During that conflict he served with the legendary 617 Dambuster Squadron. His last posting was at RAF Coningsby.

He settled in Boston on leaving the RAF in December 1948. Ralph took the town to his heart, and Boston reciprocated. He started work at G N Beaulah Ltd. in January 1949, and retired in 1989 as General Manager of Amalgamated Foods, of which Beaulah's had become part. For 20 years he was Boston Chamber of Commerce membership officer.

A cricketer of great ability, he played for both Carlton Cricket Club, and Boston Cricket Club from 1949 until he finally hung up his bat in 1974.

He has written eight previous books – of his boyhood in Jamaica, his wartime experience in the RAF and his 40 years career in wholesale grocery distribution, management.

Dudley Bryant - Publisher

Dudley Bryant

Publisher

Dudley Bryant, a true Bostonian, was born in Main Ridge, Boston, educated at Park Board School in Tunnard Street, followed by Stamford School. Having trained to become a Chartered Surveyor in Sheffield, he returned to Boston and joined the local firm of James Eley & Son, Estate Agents, Surveyors & Auctioneers in Main Ridge, becoming a Partner in 1970, and retiring in 2000.

During his career he has also been Chairman of Lincolnshire Valuers & Auctioneers, Boston Round Table & 41 Club, and a Director of Boston Chamber of Commerce. He has also been active in the Conservative Party for 40 years having been Chairman of Holland with Boston, Boston & Skegness, Lincolnshire and East Midlands. He is now President of Boston & Skegness, and still a member of various national committees.

Special Thanks

Special thanks go to Doug Moody, formerly of the Lincolnshire Standard Group and the Lincolnshire Echo, for his advice and input into the editorial content of this publication.

Preface
'Memories of Bargate in Boston'

This book follows a walking route from the northern end of the Market Place, along the pedestrianised Strait Bargate into Wide Bargate, along the western side, including Central Park and Boston Business Park, into Bargate End as far as Bargate Bridge, and returning to the Market Place via the eastern side of Wide Bargate, including Pescod Square, and Strait Bargate.

The book started from an idea from the Boston Chamber of Commerce in 2009, that I should record my memories of what I saw in Boston "business wise" in 1949 when I came to live here, and what I saw in 2009 when I retired from a lifelong career in business with Beaulah's, Amalgamated Foods and the Boston Chamber of Commerce.

It did not take long in my research to arrive at the conclusion that the amount of data would be too much for one book. Hence, the first book "Memories of Boston Market Place 1949-2009", published in 2011. This second book covers Strait Bargate, Wide Bargate up to Bargate Bridge, Pescod Square, Boston Shopping Park, and adjoining bits of adjacent streets.

In the "Market Place" book I highlighted the very important role family businesses played in the life and sustenance of the community. In general the same principle applies in this book.

In 1949 the family business names in this area of the town which come to mind are the Kitwood, Mason, Hopper, Isaac, Cammack, Robinson (Boston Standard), Giles, Holland, Coney, Beaulah, Enderby , Carr, Hutson, Lyell, Shephard, Simons, Gratton, Whites, Wing, Addy, Lingard, Nicholson, Mableson, Waterfield.

To date the family businesses which have survived are Oldrids (Isaac), Cammack & Sons, Coneys, Enderbys, Carrs, Moulders, Lyells (Dawson), Shephards (Howitt), Hutson and Hopper (now in the Market Place).

The prominent buildings were Oldrids, Red Lion Hotel, The Boston Standard offices, The General Post Office, The Boston & County Club, Cammacks, Coneys, Holland Bros, The Red Cow Hotel, J & J Beaulah's Offices, J S Towell's timber Yard, The Ram Hotel, The Cross Keys Hotel, Mill Hill, The Cattle & Sheep Market.

In the centre of the shops and offices were, and still are the open spaces of the former Cattle Market, Bargate Green, and The War Memorial.

Alas, the Cattle and Sheep Market is no longer with us, but we still have the Wednesday Auction Market, and on other days a car park.

The War Memorial remains a principal feature of Bargate, and Dudley Bryant, my publisher, and I have agreed to donate the proceeds from the sale of this book to local charities, including the upkeep of the Memorial Gardens.

Ralph Ottey

Acknowledgements
Dudley Bryant - The Publisher

Most Bostonians will agree with me that they recognise Dudley Bryant, by sight, or by name, if not both. He emits a high profile, thanks to his relationships with James Eley & Son, and the Conservative Party, locally regionally and nationally. He has either met everyone, or met the person who has met everyone. When I ring him on his mobile phone, my first enquiry is which part of the country are you in today?

We met when we were both Directors of The Boston Chamber of Commerce.

My jibe at him, is that he is responsible for the "present state of the Market Place" because he has been involved in the sale or purchase of every business property over the last 50 years.

His quick response, "Yes, but thank goodness not the Stump, nor the Assembly Rooms!"

He proudly admits to being Boston born and bred.

Our partnership, in writing this book is a follow-up from our relationship with "Memories of Boston Market Place". Taking on the task of Publisher means that he has been involved in every decision from day one. For a period of over two years, we had planning meetings on Friday mornings over coffee at the Boston & County Club, meetings at business premises, contributor's homes, Boston Library, Boston Borough Council Offices and meetings with contributors at the County Club.

He has a broad canvass of friends and acquaintances, and somehow he has cajoled them into talking, and giving personal experiences of the "Bargates".

He did all the typing, and took all the modern photographs.

It has been a privilege, and great experience, to work with him. It was also fun.

Thank you, Dudley, thank you very much.

When I asked Bostonians for help in researching this book, the response was immediate, numerous and generous. This is really a book about Bostonians by Bostonians. Listed below are the names of a few of those generous people:

Simon Hunt	Publicity Pens, typesetting, storage
Pete Foster	Ocean Digital Solutions, artwork and printing
John & Judy Cammack	Proof reading and general advice
John & Liz Hopkins	Proof reading
Neil Wright	Proof reading and specific advice
Bob & Margaret Isaac	Oldrids & Georgians
Garth Isaac	Oldrids, Georgians & Strait Bargate
Adrian Isaac	Oldrids & Strait Bargate
Andy Pottle	Manager of Pescod Square
Paul Stanney	Games Manager
David Tate	Tate's Fish Shop & Strait Bargate
George Wheatman	Journalist, Boston Standard & Target
Doug Moody	Former Group Publication Editor for 35 years of Boston Standard
Frank Cammack	Chattertons Solicitors
Brian Thornton	Carr's Funeral Service & Bargate End
Philip Towell, dec'd.	J S Towell Timber Merchants & Bargate End
Cyril Maidens	Wide Bargate
Don Holmes	Auctioneer, Cattle Market
John Clark	Bargate
Tony Ayre	Mill Hill & the Bargates
Boston Library	Susan Richardson, Sue Garn, Lisa Brown
Basil Atkin	Bargate

Sponsors

To my friends, acquaintances, well-wishers and Bostonians, I hereby publicly say a big thank you for so generously sponsoring this book.

Tony & Sheila Ayre	Retired Postman & Wife
Dennis Bambridge	Bambridges Solicitors
Brian James	Brian James, Chartered Accountant
Jean Beaulah	Housewife & Well-wisher
Rachel Beaulah	Well-wisher
Tony Cammack	Cammacks Furnishers
Matthew Carr	J. Carr & Son Ltd.
Chattertons	Boston & Lincolnshire Solicitors
David Cheung	Golden Dragon Chinese Restaurant
John & Margaret Clark	Retired Telephone Engineer & Wife
Coney's of Boston	Outfitters
Kirsty Coulson	Tip Tan Toe Beauty Salon
Dawson Butchers	Boston Family Butchers
Christine Dawson	Lyell's Boston Family Butchers
Departure Lounge Travel	Boston Travel Agents
Brian Digby	Boston Businessman
Elkington & McKay	Boston Chartered Accountants
Enderby of Boston	Optometrists & Opticians
E. Fogarty & Co.	Boston Pillow & Fabric Manufacturers
Fydell House	"Boston's Finest House"
David & Julie Hallgate	Optometrists & Opticians
Colin & Yvonne Heppenstall	Business Manager & Wife
Bernard Hibbert	Friend from Derbyshire
Tim Hopper	Hoppers the Jewellers
John & Liz Hopkins	Local Teacher & Chief Executive
Robert & Margaret Isaac	Retired Businessman & Wife
Adrian Isaac	Retired Businessman
Garth Isaac	Retired Businessman
David Ward Isaac	Retired Businessman living in Devon
Sue Johnson	Retired Physiotherapist
Delroy March	Friend from Jamaica
James & Lesley Morrison CBE	Bostonians living in London
Lancelot McFayden	Jamaican Friend, ex RAF
Peter Moulder	Moulders Dental Surgery
Fonzie Parla	Hairdresser
National Westminster Bank	Staff at Boston Branch
Lillo Parla	Hairdresser
Andy Pottle	Manager at Pescod Square
Aston Robinson	Pelo, Hairdresser
Alistair Arundel	Smart Move Ltd.
David Tate	Tate's Fish Restaurant
Tammy Smith	Time to Frame
David Waddington & Family	Boston Family living in Kent
June Jay	Retired Businesswoman

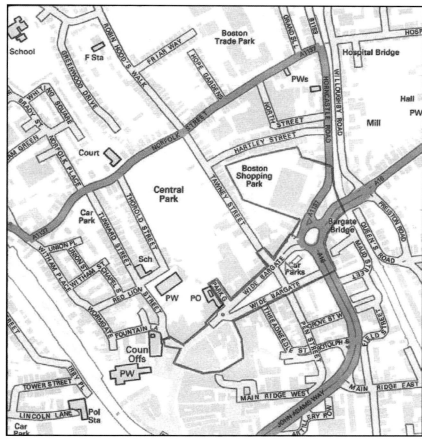
A Map of Boston Town Centre

The list of premises commences at the north end of Market Place at No.2 Strait Bargate, and follows the even numbers in a northbound direction, turning briefly into New Street, and then back along the same side of the road, following a walking route into Wide Bargate along the west side of Bargate to Bargate End, then back, returning via Bargate Bridge along the east side of Wide Bargate, back into Strait Bargate, finishing up again at its junction with Market Place.

Bargate is an important part of the shopping centre of Boston, and was also a significant area of the medieval and later town.

In medieval times, Boston was a booming town with massive exports of wool from the Port, and Boston for a few years paid more in taxes than any other town including London and Southampton. Grain, salt and lead were also exported, whilst wine was imported in large quantities.

Wide Bargate was one of the largest sheep markets in England, located just outside the historic core of Boston, and linked to the Market Place by Strait Bargate, which had important hostelries such as the Red Lion Inn, and the Falcon Inn.

Until the closure of the Cattle and Sheep Market in the 1960's there were many pubs in Wide Bargate, and a variety of commercial and small manufacturing premises, including a cigar factory, pop factory, and carriage works.

Boston's economy was built by the enterprise of many individuals and their families over the centuries, enjoying different levels of success and wealth, all being important in the development of the town, which we now inherit from them.

The bedrock of the economy has been established over the centuries, bringing us to the present day streets and buildings in the town centre, which have an amazing history.

Here, I try to record some of the modern business premises occupiers, with some notes about the families who have contributed so much to our town over so many years, and some historical snippets to add to the story.

In more recent times, these streets had many important local retailers including Oldrid, Kitwood, Mason, Bailey & Alexander and Beaulah, before the arrival and dominance of national chain retailers.

Strait Bargate was the main trunk road (A16) from Spalding to Grimsby until Bargate Bridge was widened, and re-opened in 1973. John Adams Way was built at a cost of £1.4 million, opened to traffic in 1978, and Strait Bargate was pedestrianised.

It remained traffic free until 2008 when, thanks to Lincolnshire County Council grant aid, the 'In Town' bus service - operated by Brylaine - came into being.

Incidentally, many people still refer to the area as Narrow Bargate. 'Strait' and 'Narrow' are almost identical in meaning as strait is a seafaring term for a narrow stretch of water.

2 Strait Bargate (and 61 Market Place)
Dorothy Perkins

Ladies Clothes Shop, National Company

This is now a double fronted shop, No. 61 Market Place being referred to in the "Market Place Book."

Previous occupiers of No. 2 Strait Bargate have included R. J. Harwood; Bargate Hotel and Café, whose proprietors were A.E. Scott and E. T. Austin, providing breakfasts, lunches, teas, and accommodation; Eastman Ltd., Butchers, followed by Dewhursts.

2 Strait Bargate - Dorothy Perkins

4 Strait Bargate - A. W. Curtis & Sons Ltd

4 Strait Bargate
A. W. Curtis & Sons Ltd

Bakers, a branch of the Lincoln Company

In the late 19th century until the 1930's this was occupied by George Clark, grocer, and later Reno Valet cleaners; Coombes, shoe repairs; Gullivers and Mr Mint.

6/8 Strait Bargate
Brighthouse

Furniture retailer,
National company

J. H. Small & Son, high class furniture and carpets were here in the early 1900's, followed by Star Supply stores and tea company; International tea company Stores Ltd and Mackays clothing and dress shop.

6/8 Strait Bargate - Brighthouse

10 Strait Bargate
Pandora

National chain of jewellery shops, opened in Boston, December 2014

Latterly this was Eye Candy, ladies accessories, handbags, jewellery and hats and footwear, which opened December 2013, after Jessops, the national camera chain, shut its Boston branch and after going into administration, eventually closed its entire operation.

10 Strait Bargate - Pandora

12 Strait Bargate
Cafe Nero

Coffee House, National company

Run from the 1900s to the 1960s by J. W. Tebbutt, the family drapery business. Now Pandoras and Cafe Nero it was previously Adams childrenswear.

Following on from Tebbutts, the First Floor at 2, New Street was let separately to Chartered Accountant Stephenson, Smart & Co, and then Chattertons Solicitors and Frearsons Solicitors of Skegness, who subsequently took over the Boston Solicitors business of Cooke Yarborough Swann & Cockerill in Wide Bargate.

12 Strait Bargate - Cafe Nero

Here is the entrance to New Street, leading to Red Lion Street

In the late 18th Century new houses were built and new streets were created including Witham Place,

Red Lion Street and several others behind Witham Place. Access to this development was from Strait Bargate and New Street.

It was here at the junction of Strait Bargate and New Street that Police Constable Geoffrey Denham among others used to manually direct traffic in the early 1900's.

Policing Mason's Corner

NEW STREET

1 New Street
Clarks Shoes

Shoe retailer

Today, this is all part of Clarks Shoes which stretches into Strait Bargate.

However, in the 1950s it included the Spick-and-Span cafe which featured a very popular Milk Bar. Their advert proclaimed "Always Fresh and Up To Date." Pete Allwyn was the manager, on behalf of his brother who lived in Skegness in the 1930's.

It was subsequently incorporated into Masons Shoe Shop, later becoming Clarks.

3 New Street - Argos

3 New Street
Argos

Part of Home Retail Group, market leader in the home and general merchandise market

Argos is the UK's leading digital retailer with 33,000 products, 430 million website visits and 130 million customers annually. They have 740 stores and 31,000 employees.

The original 16th Century building was home to the Falcon Inn, at that time one of the most important in the town. Later rebuilt, probably in about 1800 it then included Nos. 14-22 Strait Bargate. Owned by Soames Brewery, it was sold to Steward and Patterson in 1949. Former landlords have included Charles Taylor, Doreen and Stan Limbert, George Parrott. It was later being re-named The Boston Blitz, before closing down and demolished. The site was redeveloped for Argos.

5-9 New Street - John's Furniture

5-9 New Street
John's Furniture
Second hand retail furniture store, established 2010

This site was C. M. Johnson, wholesale drapers and floor coverings, purchased by Oldrids in 1951 and rebuilt to become Oldrids Furniture Store in 1962.
C. M. Johnson's business was transferred to the former G. N. Beaulah, wholesale grocery premises in Pump Square, when they moved to a new warehouse in Tattershall Road.

4-8 New Street
Tate's Fish Restaurant
Fish and Chips

A fish and chip service that has been available to the Boston public at the above address or thereabouts for 112 years. The present owners and controllers are the Tate family, headed by David Tate.

The Tate family are no strangers to the fish and chip business. David's parents, John and Eva, came from Yorkshire, John from a village near Ripon and Eva from Doncaster. Eva's family were deeply involved in fish and chips. They had fish and chip restaurants in Oldham, Manchester and four in Doncaster. John and Eva had two boys, Bob born in 1936 and David in 1951.

4-8 New Street - Tate's Fish Restaurant

In 1940 John enlisted in the Coldstream Guards, and along with four other soldiers, for the rest of the Second World War provided the personal guards for Prime Minister Winston Churchill, both at Chequers, the PM's official residence, and in London during the Blitz. On several occasions while Mr. Churchill was, as it were, "performing on a stage" John would be behind the curtains covering his back.

At the end of the War, John applied for a management job at a fish restaurant in London, and was promised an interview. He turned up on the appointed day, on time, only to be told that he should return the next day. Well, anyone who knew John Tate would know what his response to that would be. He told them, in no uncertain terms that he would be busy the next day. However, London's loss became Boston's gain. He applied for the manager's job at Cryer's Fish and Chip Shop and Café in Dolphin Lane, and got the job. The business was owned by Mr. Oscar Cleve, a farmer and fish merchant of Grimsby. John and Eva applied themselves to the task and built it up to what most people thought was the best fish and chip Restaurant in Boston.

In 1959, after 13 years at Cryer's, John and Eva acquired the New Street business from Mr. A. C. Evans for £3,600. The business was then run by John and Eva, and Bob. When David left Boston Grammar School in 1967 he did not join the family business, but joined Fogarty's and then Norprint.

In the 1960s and 70s, the business geography around the New Street area changed drastically. Boston Borough Council needed to straighten New Street and generally tidy up the area, so they acquired many of the small business premises adjacent to Tate's fish shop. A small triangle of buildings at the junction of New Street and Bank Street was demolished. At the age of 74, that meant the end of the career of John Richard Brown, a printer, after nearly 50 years in the same premises. He had bought the business in 1919 when he came out of the forces. Another business similarly affected was the radio and television repair service of Mr. W. Mellor. Boston and District F. C. was also displaced, and moved to Wormgate.

John Tate also acquired adjoining premises, including the former Plymouth Brethren Chapel for £2,750. As John and Eva got older, their health began to deteriorate, Bob also had an ongoing heath problem. David joined the family business in 1974. John and Eva were still involved until John suffered a stroke in 1985. Bob died in 1995, so the day to day running of the business was passed on to David. He is now assisted by Manager Sezgin Cilek (popularly known as Sam), Angie Clark (Supervisor) and other longstanding members of staff.

Eva died in 1994 and John died in 1999. David married Dawn, and has two daughters, Gemma, who has three children, two girls and a boy, and Sophie who has two sons.

The first contact I made with the Tates'[was in 1949. I was employed by G. N. Beaulah Ltd., Wholesale Grocers in Pump Square, as their Bookkeeper/Cashier, and it was part of my job to go to Lloyds Bank daily, so I walked to and fro along Dolphin Lane. One morning on my way back to the office, John Tate was outside Cryer's fish and chip shop, I had seen him before, but on this occasion he spoke to me.
"Hello friend," he said, *"I have seen you up and down the lane on many occasions. My name is John Tate. What's yours, and where do you come from?"* So, I replied *"My name is Ralph Ottey. I am from Jamaica and I work in Beaulah's office."*

He was the first person, other than my wife's family, and colleagues at work, to offer the hand of friendship. His handshake was firm, and long, and he smiled. We met and chatted on many occasions outside Cryer's in Dolphin Lane. He would greet me, *"Now then, my friend",* and I would respond *"Now then, Mr. John".*
You might think I am making a big deal out of my meeting with John Tate, but this was not the Boston of 2015, it was 1949 - over sixty years ago. Mr. James, popularly known as "Darkie" James, and I were the only black faces to be seen around town.

In 1966 I planned to take my family to Jamaica to meet my parents and family for the first time. I told John, and after some thought, he asked *"What kind of fish do they eat in Jamaica?"* I told him *"Red Tail Snapper, Goat Fish, Doctor Fish, and Mullet."*

He asked *"What about Haddock, Skate and Cod?",* And when I told him they were unheard of in Jamaica, he said if *"British Airways will allow it, I will get you the biggest Haddock in the North Sea for you to take to your family."* When I pointed out that this wouldn't be allowed, he replied *"I will make you an offer, and hope you will accept it in the spirit it is offered. As long as I have an eating place, you and your immediate family can have a meal anytime you want one."*

I accepted with thanks, but never took up the offer. The sequel came many years later, after John and Eva had passed on.

Dudley Bryant and I had been doing research for the Boston Market Place book and at mid-day I suggested lunch. Dudley said *"Let's go to Tate's."*

We went in, and after enjoying delicious fish and chips, prepared to leave. I went to David, who was on the till, and asked for the bill. He replied Ralph *"I could never charge you for a meal,"* looking to the roof, he said *"Dad would never forgive me."*

Pictured left to right: Manager, Sezgin Cilek (popularly known as Sam); Supervisor, Angie Clark; Owner, David Tate

Previously, 8 New Street has been occupied, going back to 1855, by John Cottam (hardware and toy dealer, rag and bone merchant, fancy bazaar); Munkman Robert Allen (general dealer, Smallware and marine store dealer, and Insurance agent). They moved to No. 11, Wide Bargate; Spikins Brothers (furniture and cabinet makers, Pawnbrokers and dealers).

Spikins Brothers
Furniture and Cabinet makers, prawnbrokers and dealers

The premises were then sold to engineer Samuel Hardin of Boston, for £350, and he converted it into a fish and chip shop in 1903. He was followed by George Henry Cousins; George Wilson; Thomas Frank Evans of Westwood, Ida Road, Skegness. Andrew Collin Evans purchased it for £1000 in 1935.

In the 19th and 20th Centuries there were also Morton's printers workshops, later owned by John Nickerson; Edward Odling; Herbert Odling; Nelson & Chapman; Tommy Brown, with a Solicitors office upstairs, followed by W. Mellor's electrical shop and radio and TV repairs, and charge accumulators; Boston FC Supporters Club; Jim O'Hara's Snax Club and Carlton Club; No. 8 was demolished to widen the road at Bank Street and New Street, the remainder being incorporated into Tate's. 6a New Street Boston Women's Conservative and Unionist Association and Holland with Boston Conservative and Unionist Association.

In 1973, John Tate purchased the former Plymouth Brethren Chapel on the other side of the lane at the rear to use for storage.

Fish and Chips have been fried on this site for 112 years.

14-16 Strait Bargate - Clark Shoes

14-16 Strait Bargate
Clark Shoes

National shoe retailer. Founded in 1825, based in Street, Somerset, they sell some 50 million pairs of shoes annually in 35 countries around the world.

The imposing corner property is well known as 'Mason's Corner.'

William Mason came form Kirkby on Bain. He was a Cordwainer, or bespoke shoemaker, and came to Boston in 1849, setting up business in Church Street. His son, George Herbert Mason, joined him in 1919, and the business became a retail shoe shop, as well as handmade footwear. They moved to larger accommodation at Strait Bargate in the 1890's, also living on the premises, before moving the family home to Norfolk Street.
George William Mason, and William Herbert Mason followed, then John Bryant Mason from 1946 following Army service during the war together with his brother Robert (Bob), and finally Timothy Charles Mason.
The business remained on the same site at the corner of Strait Bargate and New Street, and over the generations the property has been rebuilt and extended.
Most of that was carried out by John Bryant Mason.
The company started out by making their own shoes and boots, but as market forces changed concentrated on retailing shoes made by the leading manufacturers of the day, such as K Shoes, Clarks, Bally, Barkers, Grenson, etc. Mainly family footwear, with a very large children's department.

Under the direction of John Bryant Mason, Masons expanded, opening new shops at Lincoln, Worksop and King's Lynn, Stamford, Skegness, Worksop, Matlock. On his retirement the business was sold in 1990 to Millwood & Sons Ltd. later becoming Clarks' thus allowing Timothy to pursue his other business interests. Four generations, and a very successful business.

The building including 14-20 Strait Bargate, was rebuilt in 1933 and was set back by 10 feet to widen the footpath and roadway.

When I came to Boston in 1949, and got involved in local business, it soon became apparent that the popular consensus in family shopping was Oldrids for Drapery, Cammacks for furniture, Hoppers for jewellery, and Masons for footwear.

There was William Mason, and his son, John Bryant Mason. My first contact with John Mason was on the cricket field. He played regularly for the Old Bostonians Cricket Club in the local league, and I played for Carlton Cricket Club. He was a pace bowler, and so was I. He was a serious cricketer, and we often spent time discussing the finer points of the game. Many years later, after we both stopped playing cricket, we would meet at Boston Chamber of Commerce where John Bryant Mason would preside as President. I remember that the meetings were generally business-like, decisions precise and meetings generally short.

Later on, his younger brother Bob joined the business, and contact with him also came via the game of cricket. Bob played for Boston Town Cricket Club on Sundays (he had to be in the shop on Saturdays), and at that time I was Captain of the Carlton Cricket Club, and persuaded him to play for the Carlton.

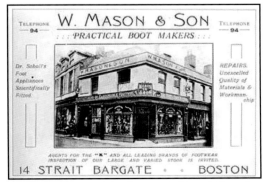

Masons of Boston giving the name to 'Mason's Corner'

John Bryant Mason

Boston League Cricket was played in the evening in Central Park, from say 5.30pm to 8pm and had very good community support. It just so happened at that time, there were two young cricketers playing in the league, and for Boston Town Cricket on Sundays, namely Bob Mason and Gerry Hopper. Bob played for the Carlton, and Gerry played for Vauxhall. They were both right handed batsmen, and were competent at playing the most dangerous shots in the game – the "hook shot". Gerry's main reason for playing cricket was to hit the ball over the trees into, or over, the houses in Thorold Street. Likewise, Bob's aim was to hit the ball on to the bowling green - feats they both accomplished on many occasions. Fortunately, no-one got hurt. In today's world, Bob Mason and Gerry Hopper wouldn't be picked to play in the Central Park, as the insurance premium would be prohibitive!!

Bob went off to run the business at Lincoln, and John's son, Timothy, joined the business at Boston. Following in father's footsteps, Tim became a Director of Boston Chamber of Commerce, and a member of the "gang of four." Young directors who were the forefront of saying Boston business must see that the Market Place must be free from rubbish. There were occasions when they literally cleaned up the Market Place after market day to show that it could be done.

The "gang of four" was Rodney Isaac of Oldrids, David Dickinson of Marks & Spencer, Tim Mason of Mason's Shoes, and Colin Rigby of Coney's gents outfitters.

Tim Mason eventually left Boston to run the store in Kings Lynn.

Here is an amazing story about Bob Mason and cricket. As I have said before, Bob could only play cricket for Boston on Sundays. On this particular Sunday, Boston was playing Worksop, a Bassetlaw League strong team. Jack Harman was Boston's captain, and one of his regular openers was unable to play. Bob Mason volunteered. Jack told him, *"You are a No. 5, Bob, the best in the business, I can't take the risk,"* whereupon Bob said, *"Bugger my eyes, Jack, all these years, I have been playing at No.5." every time I go to the wicket, the opening fast bowlers are still on, and the ball hasn't lost any of its shine."* Jack said *"Alright Bob, but just this once"*.

So, Bob opened the batting. After a few overs, he forgot he was an opener, and started playing hook shots, and hitting sixes; he was eventually caught on the boundary going for another six to make a century. He was out for 95. The following Sunday, when Bob looked at the batting order he was back at No. 5. His response was *"Maybe I will make a duck, and he will put me back at No.1."* He didn't make a duck, and he never did bat at No.1 again. Such is cricket!

The Masons have always been at the forefront of Boston's community with William Herbert Mason being a Justice of the Peace, Governor of Boston Grammar School, Rotarian, Freemason, Commissioner of Inland Revenue, Director of Chamber of Commerce. John Bryant Mason was also a JP for 28 years, Commissioner of Inland Revenue, member of HM Prison Board of Visitors at North Sea Camp, Chairman of Parole Board, Chairman of Lincolnshire Education Department Appeals Panel, Boston Round Tabler, 41 Club and Rotarian.

16 Strait Bargate

Now incorporated into Masons/Clarks Shoes, this single shop unit was separately occupied in the 1890s by C. H. Southwell, chemist, oculist and optician.

George Claypoole, the Boston jeweller and pawnbroker followed. In 1926 Stanley T. Hopper came from Goole to work for Claypoole. He subsequently took over the business, and established Hoppers the Jewellers.

There was a most impressive clock fixed to the frontage in the shape of an old fob watch. This was replaced by Mr Hopper with a more modern design and it had the reputation of being the most reliable clock in town.

During The Second World War, aircraft instruments were assembled in the upstairs workshop.

Hoppers later moved to 49 Market Place, in 1968 when Stanley's son Gerry Hopper ran the business, later to be followed by Tim and James Hopper.

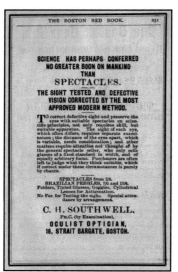
C. H. Southwell

George Claypoole Jewellers

18-20 Strait Bargate
Vision Express

Opticians. National company

Previously this has been Nelson & Co. Then came Curry's Ltd. Cycles, who were taken over by Dixon's Home Entertainments.

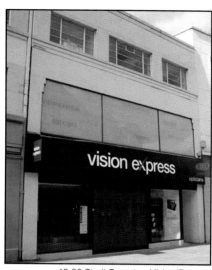

18-20 Strait Bargate - Vision Express

22 Strait Bargate - QD Stores

22 Strait Bargate
QD Stores

Retailer of general goods. National company

Originated from Norwich, a family business, which opened here in 2009, retaining four of the original Woolworth's staff.

The Red Lion Hotel

In 1515, The Red Lion Tavern was referred to as 'the Hospitium of the Red Lion in Bargate' and in 1640 was owned by the Sibsey family.

In 1794, it was bought by Sir Peter Burrell, MP for Boston, who became Lord Gardy, a founder of the MCC Cricket Club. The property was inherited by his son in 1850.

It was a famous coaching inn and posting house, where all the Boston dignitaries used to meet and do deals.

With the advent of the railways, two horse drawn buses used to take passengers from the Red Lion to the railway station.

The Red Lion Hotel

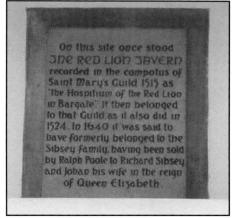

Original plaque commemorating the Red Lion

Landlords have included Matthew Enderby (1891); Charles J. Mather (1901); Sydney Lucas (1934);
Capt. A. E. Lindon MBE, (1936-1945); H. Dolton; Cyril Sykes, who grew vine tomatoes on the bowling green at the rear for sale during the wartime.

The Red Lion was also the headquarters of Boston Flying Club as well as the Red Lion Bowling Club, which is now an NCP Car Park in Red Lion Street.

Just inside the shop, high up on the right hand wall is still the original Plaque commemorating the Red Lion bearing the legend:

"On this site stood The Red Lion Tavern recorded in the compotus of Saint Mary's Guild 1515 as "The Hospitium of the Red Lion in Bargate." It then belonged to that Guild as it also did in 1524. In 1640 it was said to have formerly belonged to the Sibsey family having been sold by Ralph Poole to Richard Sibsey and Johan his wife in the reign of Queen Elizabeth".

To illustrate the social standing of the Red Lion Hotel in the 1940's/50's, I will tell you a tale from my late father-in-law, Arthur Reece. He had a friend, a Mr. Horry, who had a small market garden business in the Mount Bridge area. One day he and Mr. Horry met in the Market Place. Out of the blue, Mr. Horry said:-

"Arthur, guess what? I recently went into the Red Lion, and who do you think I saw in the Lounge having drinks with cherries in? James Reid (a substitute name, I assure you). Where does he get his money from?"   "Where indeed was his response?."

You see Mr. Reid was a labourer in the Railways Goods Yard.

The Red Lion was demolished in 1959 and rebuilt for F W Woolworth & Co., Ltd., who moved from across the road, and remained here till they closed in 2009.

Former Woolworths

24-26 Strait Bargate - New Look

24-26 Strait Bargate

New Look

National ladies' clothing, shoes and accessories

Originally, this was two shops.

24 Strait Bargate

William Barton

Inventor of Premier Stoves, and attended Paris Exhibition in 1882. He was an ironmonger. On his death the business was purchased by Holland Bros., also ironmongers, being succeeded by Hutson Bros., whose story is recounted later at 11 Wide Bargate. The Holland Brothers story is told at 26A Wide Bargate.

Following Hutson's, this shop was, amongst others, R. N. Chapman Carpets, Philip Clift, ladies outfitter; Joan Burns Ltd., Skirts, blouses, knitwear and hosiery specialists, plus prams and toys, throughout the 1930s to 1960s. Followed by Eastern Carpet Stores. By 1984 it was Bambers Ladieswear, Fosters Menswear.

Next door at 24A Strait Bargate from 1930s - 1960s was J. H. Smith & Sons, dry cleaners before they moved to 8 Wide Bargate.

26 Strait Bargate

In 1891 this was Arthur Holland, hatter, followed by Thomas. H. Bailey, hatter and hosier in 1893. Tom Bailey was the only hat manufacturer in the county, advertising himself as 'Wholesale and Retail hat and cap warehouse' with 'A choice of Paris and Felt hats always in stock. School caps, Livery and Gentlemen's standard shape hats. Made to order on shortest notice. The trade liberally treated with." From 1886 to 1995 it was continued by Arthur Holmes Holland.

From 1930's to the 1960's it was Lipton's Ltd., grocers, then Visionhire TV and Preedy the newsagents and greeting cards, owned by Maurice Parker of Grantham.

Adjacent was Parkers Passage leading to the Men's Own Club/Temperance Club, which later moved to the Mason's Arms in Silver Street.

28-30 Strait Bargate

Currently vacant, recently occupied by Evans ladies wear, national ladies clothing, shoes and accessories which opened in about 1992 and closed down in January 2015, moving into Oldrids Department Store.

Originally this appears to have been two shops and at times occupied by J & J Beaulah, Oldrid & Co., Drapers, Kwick cleaners and also Wakefield's Army and Navy Stores.

When Josiah and Minnie Beaulah and family went on holiday to Wales in the 1900's, Josiah would send the children into local shops to ask for Beaulah's Canned Peas, in the hope that they would later receive enquiries for the product.

John Beaulah went into partnership with Mr. Alfred Reynolds as wholesale grocers until the 1880's, when Mr. Reynolds founded his own business and John brought his younger brother Josiah in as a partner.

J & J Beaulah started in 28 Strait Bargate as wholesale and retail grocers, then branched out into canning in Wide Bargate in the late 19th century. In the early 1930s, the business was split with Wilfred Beaulah taking the canning business to premises at Bargate End. Gerald Beaulah retained the grocery under his name, G. N. Beaulah Ltd. Subsequently moving to Pump Square. By 1939 this was Houghton & Kempton Ltd. Dyers and Cleaners, followed by Kwick Cleaners. The shop and rear premises, formerly the Men's Own Club, were later purchased by Oldrids, who occupied it as a drapery and carpet shop in 1950s to 1970s. When the second phase of Oldrids rebuilding was completed in 1971, the carpets and soft furnishings departments moved into the new store, and Oldrids subsequently sold these premises to Jimmy Goldsmith, who planned to demolish it together with neighbouring Lipton's and Sketchley's to build a supermarket, but he subsequently scrapped the idea.

Valentine's Bananas rented the old club building before moving to 51 Wide Bargate, next to the New England Hotel.

It appears that for much of the time, these two properties have been in the same ownership, as they have varied between occupations by either one or two different companies.

32-34-36 Strait Bargate

Now partly vacant. Until recently Age UK Boston & South Holland operated this as a Community Hub before moving to Bank House, 116 High Street.

32 Strait Bargate

The original No. 32 was occupied over the years by Strait Bargate by Mrs. Kowskie, confectioner; also followed by Elijah Dowlman, confectioner; Charles William Newton, baker; J. Swain; Visionhire TV; Granada TV Rental; Card Fair, cards and gift.

34 Strait Bargate

Similarly there have been a number of occupiers from 1891. Birch, fancy goods; 1901 John Beedall, draper; 1934 Weaver-to-Wearer Ltd., Tailors.

36 Strait Bargate

From 1840's to 1890's this was Tom Kitwoods, grocer and baker.

In the 1890' and 1900's, this was John Beedall, draper and milliner. He was a native of Sibsey, starting business in 1897 at Horncastle. In 1894 he opened up on this imposing corner site as a draper and milliner 'for the people at popular prices for cash.'

Later, in the 1930's this became A. B. Woodcock's bakery and pastry cook, run by head baker Mr. Lee, the owner having been killed in Wide Bargate.

Then in 1950's this corner site was rebuilt and became Sketchley's Dry Cleaners and SupaSnaps, until it closed in 2009.

Just before publication, this corner shop has re-opened as Eye Candy, taking larger premises than their previous shop at 10 Strait Bargate.

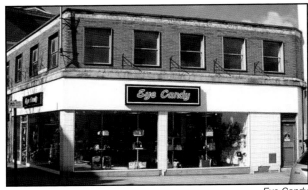

Eye Candy

These properties were bought by Sir James Goldsmith of Allied Foods with a view to redevelopment, together with Sketchley's. The vision was to redevelop this frontage and adjoining premises in Wide Bargate with land at the rear into a major shopping area in competition with the proposal for Pescod Square. It never happened, but Pescod Square did. Even today the whole site frontage together with the Red Lion Street car park is for sale, if you want to buy it, at £3.25 million.

WIDE BARGATE

Wide Bargate was originally developed with substantial residential properties for the leading citizens of Boston and over the years they have been turned into various shops, offices, etc.

4 Wide Bargate

4 Wide Bargate
Icon

Hairdresser, tattoos, beauty therapy, spray tanning.
Opened in 2011 and closed in 2014.

In 1896 this was the offices of James Eley, auctioneer, surveyor, estate agent and agricultural valuer.

Dr Richard Kime Allday, who was born at this address, recalls his family life:

In 1923, Charles Richard Allday (1890-1949) came from Birmingham to Boston to set up a dental practice, and purchased 4 Wide Bargate.

The ground floor was the dental surgery and workshop, and the upper floors became the family home.
He married the daughter of Fred Kime, fish merchant of Assembly Rooms, Market Place, Boston, and on 11 June 1923, Richard Kime Allday was born at 4 Wide Bargate.
Richard attended Conway Primary School in Boston and then went to boarding school at Taunton in Somerset in 1937.

During the Second World War the Allday family was evacuated to Lower Asholt, between Taunton and Bridgewater. Richard's two sisters were educated at Kings College, Bridgewater, and his younger brother was born in Poole, Dorset - Aged 16 years Richard Allday recalls that he was caught smoking by his father whilst waiting at the bus stop on London Road. He was in terrible trouble!

Dental Surgeon Stanley H Pollard LDS, RCS, also practised from 4 Wide Bargate in 1939.

The Allday family returned to Boston in 1941 to live at London Road (just beyond Tytton Lane East), and Charles Richard Allday continued to practice dental surgery at 4 Wide Bargate.
After leaving school Richard had various jobs from a packer at LINCAN to Alliance Assurance Company, and working for his father in the dental workshop.

Lionel C. Purnell joined the dental practice at 4 Wide Bargate, and on the death of Charles Richard Allday he brought in to the practice John F. Leake. They remained here until the dental practice moved to Pen Street.
Lionel and Dorothy Purnell were both serving in the Royal Army Dental Corps (RADC), and were posted to India.
In about 1940, Dorothy travelled to India via the Mediterranean Sea, to be followed six months later by husband Lionel who had to sail via the Cape of Good Hope due to the war in the Mediterranean.

When the war ended, they returned to the UK and looked for a job. Similarly, John F. Leake was also serving in the RADC in India, and they both ended up in Boston with C. R. Allday at 4 Wide Bargate. John Leake was recalled to serve with the Gloucestershire Regiment during the Korean War, later returning to Boston.
On the death of C. R. Allday, Lionel Purnell had been left as the only dentist, but Howard Leake who was trained as a dentist at Guy's Hospital, London and called up to do National Service in the RADC from 1959 to 1961. Thus the potential of four dentists in practice together including Michael Purnell up and coming, larger premises were needed, so the old Blind Home at 25, Pen Street, was purchased at auction. The Blind Home moved to "Sunniholme", Tower Road. Michael joined the Army and trained as a dentist, then joined the Pen Street practice until his retirement.
Richard K Allday served in the Royal Navy during the Second World War, and on his 21st Birthday was in Hiroshima following the dropping of the first atom bomb.
After the war, he obtained a grant to study medicine at Guys Hospital Medical School, qualifying in 1953, then practicing as a locum doctor south of London, and in Gainsborough and elsewhere.
After his marriage in 1949, he returned to Boston, working in the medical practice of Sheehan, Pankhurst and Brackenridge at 75 High Street, Boston (now flats fronting on to High Street at the corner of Liquorpond Street). Dr. Sheehan invited him to become a partner, but the other partners did not agree, so Dr. Sheehan left the partnership and started a new practice with Dr Richard Allday, known as Sheehan & Allday in Liquorpond Street. in new premises were built on the site of cottages which had been destroyed by bombs (the present day offices of Lister & Co and Gerry Smith), and are opposite the present Liquorpond Street Surgery and the Co-Op Pharmacy.
Dr. Allday retired from the medical partnership in 1985, but continued to practice medicine as a locum until 1990.
Over the years, the practice expanded with additional doctors being introduced, including Drs. Tyrer; Wookey; Cooper; Kirk-Smith; Brocklehurst; Germer; Rance; Matiti; Nolan; Fernandes; Moore; Ramana; and Ralalage.
Many Bostonians will remember buying books from Dr. Allday's shop in High Street, Kay Books, initially to sell Richard Kay's publications, and in particular the "History of Boston Series". His daughter, Becky, now continues the business as an online bookshop www.kaybooksonline.co.uk
Other medical practitioners working from 4 Wide Bargate have included Dr. A Eckford; Dr. R G Flower; Dr. P D Bennett.
There have been several occupiers here during recent times, including Bonds of Boston, furnishers; In Touch cards and Gifts; Cupid cards and gift shop; Everyday Essentials, household goods and various short term tenants of the premises.

6 Wide Bargate

Archway Passage access to the rear and
Red Lion Street Car Park

6 Wide Bargate is actually the archway leading to the rear of 4 & 8 Wide Bargate and now the Red Lion Street Car Park and previously the Lincolnshire Standard printing works.

8 Wide Bargate
Oxfam

National charity shop.

Established at least 20 years ago.
In 1893, this was the premises of Miss S. A. Strawson, fancy dealer.

8 Wide Bargate - Oxfam

In 1930's it became Clarke & John Davison, outfitters, followed by Henry Cooke, high class fruiterer, floral decorations, bouquets and fresh cut flowers. Then in 1960's it was Smiths dry cleaners.

10 Wide Bargate
Thomson Travel

National Travel Agents.

G. Henderson, baker and confectioner was here in 1893, becoming Henderson's Bakery, then G. A. Gray, confectioner and baker in the 1950's

In the 1960's it became Rentaset, television hire; Radio Rentals; followed by Ellerman Travel and Lunn Poly Travel Agents.

Thomson Travel

Co-Operative Food Supermarket

12 Wide Bargate
Co-Operative Food Supermarket

Previously Somerfield's, convenience store, National Company.

These premises had also been occupied by Skegness Pottery Company and Thrifty (Marks and Spencer seconds retailer) and Choices video rentals, before becoming Somerfield's.

But this building is historically known as the home of one of the most well-known local businesses in Boston, the Boston Standard.

The Boston & Lincolnshire Standard was established in 1912 by the Conservative MP for Horncastle, Sir Archibald Weigall, who lived at what is now the Petwood Hotel at Woodhall Spa, together with a group of Conservatives who thought it necessary to have a weekly newspaper dedicated to the Conservative cause and to counter-balance the efforts of the effective Liberal newspaper, the Boston Guardian.

In 1911 an executive committee was set up, and some 2000 shareholders enrolled.
The formative directors were Ben Simons of Willoughby, an Auctioneer and Valuer; F. E. Bowser of Wigtoft, C. H. Dixon of Holbeach; T.E Dennis, Agriculturalist of Kirton; H.P. Carter of Oakham; W.S. Royce of Pinchbeck, and MP for Boston; the Hon. R.P. Stanhope of Revesby Abbey.
Capt. Weigall appointed the first editor, George Robinson, the then editor-manager of the Lincolnshire Chronicle at Lincoln.

Original premises were at 12 Threadneedle Street, from where the first edition of the newspaper was published on 6th July 1912.

But just two years after the first issue hit the streets came the outbreak of the First World Ward which saw many of the staff called up for military service.

In 1920, the company bought the Georgian house at 12 Wide Bargate with its large garden from Dr. Reginald Tuxford, physician and surgeon, which during the war had been used by the Ministry of Food. The large garden at the rear was developed into the printing works, together with part of the Central Park purchased from the Council. This property became synonymous with Bargate for some 70 years, remaining there until 1974, when the printing operation moved to Redstone Industrial Estate, and a shop opened in Church Lane, near St. Botolph's Footbridge where it remains, although the printing has long since left Boston.

It is fair to say that under the leadership of George Robinson, and his son, Lionel, the company grew through acquisition and merger to an almost monopolistic position in Lincolnshire. It also changed its political stance, no longer the mouthpiece of the Conservative Party, but published news and comment as it thought fit.

More titles were launched and other newspapers taken over, and The Lincolnshire Standard Group eventually had publications covering most of the County and South Humberside, including Lincoln, Gainsborough, Scunthorpe, Grimsby, making it one of the biggest independently owned newspapers in the country.

I was privileged to share a classroom with Lionel Robinson at Pilgrim College, Fydell House, in the 1950's at a night school studying the 1916 Russian Revolution. Mr. Robinson was the most senior student, and I do remember his skirmishes with the lecturer from Nottingham University. He would question, examine, and sometimes cross examine him. Later, in the 1960s, I was a student at Pilgrim College with his son Tony Robinson in Alan Champion's Philosophy classes, and he would question, examine and cross examine Alan just like his father.

The Chairman of Directors was John Simons, Principal of Simons estate agents and Auctioneers, followed by Tony Tunnard, Solicitor of Jebb and Tunnard, in 1975.

The Robinson dynasty came to an end in the 1990s after three generations - George Robinson retired in 1951, was succeeded by his son, Lionel, and then his grandson, Anthony - when LSG was taken over by the Canterbury based Adscene Group owned by Harry Lambert. In 1999 he sold to Southnews, who then sold it to the Johnson Publishing Ltd. in May 2000.

George Wheatman recalls researching angling news from Albert Morley, of Morley sports shop for Wilf Berry's *"Tommy Ruffe Angling"* column in the days when the Standard's sports coverage was dominated by bowls, Boston United Football Club and angling. When Boston United played away mid-week, supporters used to crowd into Wide Bargate to see the half-time scores placed in the Standard front office window. On publication day, queues would spill out into Bargate as people waited for the paper to come off the press.

The years since the Standard was first published have seen many changes, not only in the technical development in the production of the newspaper but also in the lifestyle of its readers.

When the paper was launched the telephone, the car and the aeroplane were comparative rarities. There was no radio, no radar, no television, no domestic electricity and no home central heating. And things like computers, mobile phones and space travel were mere figments of the imagination.

During the strike of 1921, a tractor was brought into the works department and provided the power for the printing press during the emergency. Mr. D. T. Gratton, the founder of Gratton's the agricultural engineers who were also based in Bargate, masterminded it.

Some years after the Second World War, around 1951, expansion brought the need for more accommodation. On inspection of two disused rooms at the top of the Wide Bargate premises, what appeared to be two scorch marks were noticed on the ceiling. When prodded with a broom handle the whole area disintegrated and crashed to the floor.

Investigation revealed that an incendiary bomb had penetrated the roof, slid down a joist and ended lying on its side trapped in the angles of the supports. In the process of burning itself out, the incendiary had eaten its way through several inches of heavy timber. That was the extent of the damage – but a lucky escape!
It was only in 1962, on the occasion of the newspaper's golden jubilee, that news appeared on the front pages. Previously this prime position had been entirely given over to advertising.

In 1970, the old letterpress method of printing was replaced by web offset (lithography) printing. This enabled the Standard to become a two-section newspaper. Three years later came the change to complete photocomposition and paste up techniques better suited to the highly developed production system.
Twenty one years later, on 30th January 1981, the Standard got a bright new look. Gone forever was the unwieldy broadsheet newspaper and in its place readers were able to enjoy a new look tabloid which was easier to read and much easier to handle.

With the demise of the printing department at Boston, the old Goss press which had ruled for more than 40 years stopped printing for the last time. But it didn't go quietly. During its demolition a spark from oxyacetylene equipment caused a serious fire in the pressroom. The whole building was evacuated and Boston Fire Brigade spent several hours extinguishing the fire and the smouldering timbers of the building. The inside of the press was severely damaged but the building remained structurally intact.

The Standard has always been proud of its reputation of being what is known in the industry as a "family newspaper" – one that can go into any home and be read by all without fear of the content causing concern.

But at the Bargate headquarters "family" has been at the heart of the operation since the first Standard edition hit the streets.

Lincolnshire Standard

At boardroom level there were, over the years, the Simons, Bateman and Tunnard family connections.

Gerard H. Periam returned to the Standard after some years working for the East Midlands Allied Press in Peterborough to become managing editor in 1970, retiring three years later.

Charles Hall was deputy editor and also one of the country's most respected agricultural journalists and Dick Ryan was news editor, followed by Ted Coleman and Norman Bainbridge.

Others occupying the editor's chair over the years have been Bob Lenton; George Wheatman a popular former sports editor and one of the founders members of Boston Sports Council; and Geoff O'Neil now working in local government as head of communications for South Kesteven District Council and who is also the current chairman of Boston Rugby Club.

Doug Moody was group production editor responsible to managing directors Lionel, and later, Anthony Robinson. He later worked for the Lincolnshire Echo as a content editor.

And of course, there was the late Wilfred Berry whose career with the Standard spanned 60 or more years. He started work in the newspaper's early days as a linotype operator then moved into the editorial department as sports editor. Apart from covering all the Boston United games – he never tired of talking about the FA Cup game when United travelled to London to face the might of Tottenham Hotspur at White Hart Lane after beating Derby County in a previous round – his bowls column "Without Bias" and his "Angling with Tommy Ruffe" feature were avidly read by the town's sporting fraternity.

In the newsroom could be found the late Allan R. Eves a multi-talented journalist who was the Standard's municipal correspondent and a columnist who wrote without fear or

favour on issues, often thorny political matters and sometimes light-hearted, affecting the town and its residents.

In the editorial department news reporter and women's feature specialist Pat Ashberry

found herself working alongside son Jeremy, as did news editor Pam Browne and her son Duncan, the current Standard sports editor.

But of the many editorial members of the Standard team over the years, probably the name that is known to most readers is that of Gary Atkinson. The former chief photographer, who still lives in the town, was known to literally thousands of people who had been on the 'other side' of his camera lens.

Other names, which will strike a chord, are the late Norman Revell, who was group advertising manager and also well known for his work with the Boston Lions Club – as was former group administrator Owen Moorin also a classical musician of note.

In the press hall the Meeds family held sway. From the first day, the first machine manager was Jim Meeds snr and on his retirement his son Jim – still a familiar face in the town – took over the role and was in charge of the press until its demise. He was later production manager for some years.

Another character in the printing works was chief stone hand Alf Peatling who, with his team, was responsible for making up the news and classified pages. Son David followed him into the industry, starting as an apprentice and when he left after over 40 years service was keyboard supervisor and heavily involved in the new production technology.

David, incidentally, was well known as one of the disc jockeys at the famous Boston Gliderdrome during its halcyon days and later wrote a book on those glory years called 'Going to the Dance".

14 Wide Bargate
William H. Brown

National estate agents and auctioneers.

William H. Brown, auctioneers and estate agents was established in 1896 by William H. Brown offering an auctions and valuation service from a hut in a stack yard at Ruskington. Over the years they have expanded into a group of some 110 branch offices.

The Boston branch originally occupied the first floor offices, and subsequently expanded into the ground floor shop, where they are today.

The principal partners of William H. Brown latterly were Michael Brown and Tony Snarey, who sold out to Royal Insurance.

William H Brown

In earlier times, this once a private house was occupied by John Morton, printer and Charles Adelsee, professor of music. Then in the 1900s it became Ranshaw and Lambert, costumier and dressmakers; Dr. R. Tuxford; G. A. Brough, ladies outfitter in the 1950s, and Clark's of Retford, dry cleaners in 1960s.

Target Newspaper

16 Wide Bargate
Target Newspaper

Local newspaper, part of Lincolnshire Echo Group.

The Target was launched as a free newspaper in 1984 in High Street premises, followed by first floor offices above Phones 4 U in Strait Bargate. It moved to Wide Bargate 10 years later. The industry 'experts' predicted that the new baby would not last 6 months, in what was a cut throat business. The first Editor was George Wheatman and the Bargate premises were opened by the then Mayor, Cllr. Keith Dobson.

The Target celebrated its 30th birthday in 2014, and George Wheatman, now in retirement, is still writing his popular column. The paper became one of the big successes in Lincolnshire's newspaper history, with editions being added to most parts of the County.

The premises had been converted for occupation by the Target, but the Strongroom of previous occupiants Barclays Bank was so well built in that it had to remain in situ.

George Wheatman

Records show this property also having been the home of Joseph Lightfoot, farmer in 1890; Alfred Reynolds, auctioneer, followed in the early 1900's as the offices Jebb and Tunnard, solicitors. In the 1950's and 60's the Senior Partner was R.A.C. Tony Tunnard, who was also Chairman of Lincolnshire Standard Group, and Clerk to Black Sluice Internal Drainage Board. Jebb and Tunnard eventually moved to 5 Main Ridge, next to the Masonic Temple, now being known as Sills and Betteridge, Solicitors.

Martins Bank Ltd. Were next to occupy 16 Wide Bargate and the Manager was Don Sargeant of Woodhall Spa. Martins were incorporated into Barclays Bank, who purchased to 700 branches of Martins, and sold the building to Boston Target.

18 Wide Bargate
Post Office

Recently closed down, and moved to be incorporated into W. H. Smith's shop at 27 Strait Bargate.

The Boston Post Office was originally in High Street, and moved here in 1907, when a private house on the site was demolished to make way for the new General Post Office.

18 Wide Bargate

This head post office is one of the most imposing buildings in Boston, built on three floors and extending to over 16,000 square feet of floor area. It provided accommodation not only for the Post Office, but also the telephone exchange, sorting office and vehicle maintenance, and also served 73 sub branches around Lincolnshire. There were three daily letter postal deliveries from Monday to Friday, at 7am, 9.45am and 4pm. It was ceremonially opened by the Postmaster General, the Rt. Hon. Sydney C. Buxton JP. Postmasters have included Mr. Hudson and Mt. Rainbow. There was no ceremony when it closed in 2014.

The whole property is now vacant, and advertised for sale at £850,000 with planning consent for the rear to become a restaurant and the upper floors to be converted in to 10 residential units, whilst retaining a shop on the corner at ground level at the front.

Park Gate, the entrance to Central Park and the Boston & County Club Ltd

Here is Park Gate, and the Entrance to Central Park, and the Boston & County Club.

20 Wide Bargate - Prezzo

20 Wide Bargate
Prezzo

Italian Restaurant, National Company.

This historic and imposing property was previously known as "Park House"; "Tunnard House"; "Hopkins House"; Oldrid's Park; "Conway House"; "Boston & District Agricultural Club"

It was the home of Samuel Tunnard (1750-1818), lawyer, who built the original house in 1790. At that time the population of Boston was about 6,000, and the Borough contained about 8,000 acres.
The "garden" of Tunnard's house was about 20 acres, the equivalent of a quarter percent of the whole of Boston. This "garden" at the rear was a deer park and became known as "Tunnard's Park", and included what is now Tawney Street, an ice house where Bush Tyres are now, the present Tunnard Street, Hartley Street, and Park Board School which was demolished to become a public car park in Tunnard Street, Thorold Street and Tawney Street.

The Tunnard family once owned nearly all of Boston and Frampton.

Having started a law practice in Boston in 1775, Samuel Tunnard then built an adjoining office, at 22 Wide Bargate in 1795. In modern times this legal practice became Jebb and Tunnard, now Sills and Betteridge in Main Ridge West.

His daughter married Richard Thorold of Weelsby House, Grimsby at the fashionable St. George's, Hanover Square, London.

In 1825, the house was let to Thomas Hopkins, Solicitor, who founded the law practice in Main Ridge, later known as Rice, Waite and Marris, and now Morley Brown and Co.

In the late 19th Century it became home of John Oldrid the Second and the Oldrid family, the grounds then becoming known as "Oldrid's Park" and continuing to extend to some 20 acres.

In 1894, other properties in his ownership fronting Wide Bargate and the large park to the north were divided between the Central Park and residential development along the present day streets.

By 1904, the property was described as "a mansion or dwellinghouse in Wide Bargate with domestic offices and other outbuildings and yards, gardens and park extending to 11 acres, 2 roods, and 25 perches occupied by Mrs. Oldrid".

In the early 1900s it became the boarding house of Conway High School. Head Mistress was Miss Mary Alice Stothert, and there were six resident mistresses, 12 visiting masters, and 150 scholars, including 40 boarders.

Central Park, formerly known as "Tunnard's Park", "Hopkins Park", and "Oldrid's Park", was purchased by the Corporation in 1919 to become the town's main recreational space, where regular games of bowls, cricket and tennis were enjoyed by numerous people in friendly competition.

Sadly, these sporting facilities are no longer available, but the Park remains a rare green open space in the town centre now used for simple recreation, and occasional entertainments and shows in the heart of the town, and enjoyed by all.

In 1919, Nos. 20 and 22 Wide Bargate were sold by Connolly Norman Tunnard to Boston and County Club Ltd. It adjoined premises owned by George Holland (Holland Bros. Garage), Benjamin Simons (auctioneer), and the Park.

No. 20 became what is known as "The County Club", a private member's club, its objects being "To maintain and conduct a social club, and to provide a club house and other conveniences for the use of the members of the club and their friends."

The seven founding Directors were Frederick Ezekiel Bowser, farmer, Wigtoft; Joseph Bowser, farmer, Frithville; Alexander Francis, merchant, Boston; William Gilding, farmer and merchant, Swineshead; Arthur Ingamells, auctioneer and estate agent, Boston; William Edward Pearson, farmer and merchant, Freiston; Edwin Welsh, farmer, Leverton, together with Alfred de Bouys Johnson (Johnson's Seeds Director); Percy Ostler (timber salesman);Thomas Harold Balderston (auctioneer); Albert Wright (butcher); together with numerous farmers including Arthur Saul, Thomas Henry Richardson, Sydney Roberts, John Robert Cannon, Alfred Tunnard, Charles Gilliatt Kendrick and Richard Hardy.

Hence, it was then became known as "The Farmers' Club", and two of the former stewards were Hugh Archibald McDowell, and Arthur Spensley, known as Bert.

The Club Rules stated that all members shall be of good social position. Lady members shall not be entitled to attend or vote at any meetings of the club, nor be eligible to serve on a committee or wine committee. They shall be entitled to use such parts of the clubhouse as are set apart for their exclusive use by the committee, and it became very popular as a Gentlemen's Club, especially on Wednesday market days.

In 1965 the Boston and County Club sold the frontage building of Nos. 20 and 22 Wide Bargate to the East Midlands Trustee Savings Bank, whose Head Office was at No. 33 Market Place, Boston, and its Trustees were then Harold Colquhoun Marris (Solicitor); Harry Bateman (brewer); John Conbro Mossop (solicitor); and John Stanley Maples (solicitor).

At the time, No. 22 had been held on lease by Royal Insurance Company for 10 years. The sale price was £65,000, which enabled the County Club to build new and modern single storey club premises at the rear on the site of their bowling green, adjacent to the entrance to Central Park, and this is where the club continues to flourish today.

Boston & County Club Ltd

Royal Insurance subsequently moved to the former TSB premises at 33 Market Place.

Trustee Savings Bank were then taken over by Lloyds Bank, becoming Lloyds TSB, which eventually closed down, and these two properties are now Prezzo and PAB Translation Centre.

Today, all has changed at the Boston and County Club, and since May 1991, lady members have become a welcome addition to the well-being of the Club, and it prospers with snooker, bridge, members' events, as well as being host to regular meetings of Rotary, Ladies MacMillan, Ladies Luncheon, Portcullis, Boston Conservatives Supper Club, all enjoying the facilities and catering provided.

Modern day Club Presidents have included Peter Pocklington (1989-1996); Harry Clarke (1996-1997); Bob Tunnard (1997-2005); Philip Harris (2005 – present day).

The Club has become a major venue for private non-member celebrations and functions including weddings christenings, birthdays, etc.

22 Wide Bargate
PAB Translation Centre

Chartered members of the Chartered Institute of Linguists. Winner of 'Best Contribution to Boston Awards' 2010.

Translation service for over 200 languages.

Having originally been built by Samuel Tunnard as his office, it was separated from next door to eventually become Read and Sutcliffe, ship brokers, who moved to office premises on Boston Docks. It was then Skinner's Financial Service until 2009.

22 Wide Bargate - PAB Translation Centre

BOSTON MEMORIAL GARDENS AND BOSTON CENOTAPH

Located opposite the former Post Office, believed to be on land originally acquired by Boston Corporation in 1601 as part of a 4 acre site in Wide Bargate, and now remembering the fallen from both the First and Second World Wars.

In 1919, the Army Council made available to towns with a population exceeding 10,000, 'war relics' to permanently commemorate the notable achievements of its citizens in financing the war, and bear testimony to the important part played by the Boston War Savings Committee. From 1916 to 1919 a grand total of £2,200,000 in savings of War Securities, War Bonds, and War Savings Certificates was achieved.

The cannons, Bargate Green — which had been captured at Sebastopol during 1854-5 and presented to the town after the Crimean War. They were later joined by the First World War tank but were destroyed for scrap metal during the Second World War. One of the shops along Bargate was that of E. W. Peakome, a local photographer who produced postcards. He is next door to Wilkinson and Son. The message on the postcard says 'In the background, to the left of the cannons, is Mr. White's of Boston, where I was married'.

The Crimean Cannons

An English First World War Mark IV 30 ton 'female' tank, manufactured by Fosters of Lincoln and having operated with six Lewis machine guns, and 24,000 rounds of ammunition, was delivered to Boston and received by Mayor Alderman A. Cooke-Yarborough in the Market Place. It was moved to its display site at Bargate Green to sit alongside the two 36 pounder Russian cannons from the Crimean War, captured at Sebastopol in 1854-55. They were presented to the Town in 1856 by the War Office.

Later a captured 18 pounder German field gun was added to the display.

The present day memorial, Boston Cenotaph, was an idea first proposed by George William Ingram, seed merchant of 27 Market Place, and John Watson Loveley, Baker & Confectioner, from which the War Memorial Committee was established to raise the funds to pay for it. A sum of £2,800 was raised by public subscription and as the cost was £2,200, the balance was donated to the Boston Hospital Committee to provide beds for ex-servicemen.

A magnificent structure, it standing 28 feet high, the Cenotaph was designed by W. S. Wheatley FRIBA, and built by Samuel Sherwin and Son of Wide Bargate, Boston. It is made of Portland stone with Hopton stone panels.

The present day memorial, Boston Cenotaph

Memorial unveiled on 25th September, 1921

This Memorial was unveiled on 25th September 1921 by the Earl of Yarborough, the Lord Lieutenant of Lincolnshire. The original inscription read: *"To the Glory of God and in grateful remembrance of the Men of Boston who gave their lives in the Great War 1914"*.

It remembers 348 young men, mainly from the Lincolnshire Regiment and Boston Rifles.

This inscription has since been covered by the bronze cast of Boston people killed in the Second World War. By 1935 it was considered the 'war relics' no longer held any significance, and there was a suggestion that they be replaced with a statue of the 19th century local poet, Jean Ingelow. The Lincolnshire Standard campaigned vigorously for their removal, and following the unveiling of the Cenotaph many considered these 'war relics' to be ugly monstrosities, and superfluous.

In 1937 Boston Borough Council sold the Second World War tank and German field gun for £56 to Thos. W. Ward Ltd of Sheffield as scrap metal. The cannons remained until 1940 when they were sold for an undisclosed sum as part of the scrap salvage scheme for armaments manufacture in the Second World War.

In 1949, a bronze tablet remembering the fallen in the Second World War was added to the south west face of the Cenotaph covering the original inscription.

In 1994 the railings to hold the wreaths were added to the base of the Cenotaph, being a gift from local engineering firm Craven and Nicholas of Dock Road, Boston, in remembrance of the company founder's son, Douglas Nicholas.

The modern forged steel sculpture archway at the entrance from Wide Bargate was added in 1995, being designed by Matthew Fedden of Gloucestershire. It stands five metres high, weighs over 2 tons and cost £9,050.

'Veterans Way'

Veterans Way Plaque

'Walk in this Garden of Peace and Remember'

In 2006, the Dunkirk, Normandy and Merchant Navy Veterans requested that plaques be commissioned for their fallen members and installed in the Gardens. A committee was formed to organise the project.

The Memorial Gardens was established, and now has 56 individual memorial plaques in place which include:-

Allied Armed Forces and Civilians throughout Europe 1939-1945
The Pioneer Corps and Royal Pioneer Corps
1st. Para Division, OP "Market Garden", Arnhem. September 1944
Royal Corps of Signals Certa Cito
Lancaster Bomber crews who flew over this town from local bases during World War Two
1st Air landing Light Regiment Royal Artillery
Queen Alexandra's Royal Naval Nursing Service; Princess Mary's Royal Air Force
Nursing Service; Queen Alexandra's Royal Army Nursing Corps.
Royal Army Service Corps and Royal Corp. Transport
Royal Navy and Royal Marine Crews in Landing Craft, 'Combined Operations'
Hindoostan Royal Leicestershire Regiment
Royal Anglian Regiment
Malaya and Borneo Veterans Association
Royal Naval Association
OBIQUE, Royal Artillery
Royal Air Force
Royal Engineers
ATS (Donated by Women's Royal Army Corps Association)
Royal Naval Patrol Service
Merchant Navy
1st Army Djebels Association - "Operation Torch"
The Canal Zoners Association 1950-1957
British Korean War Veterans 1950-1953
Special Forces, Special Operations Executive 1940-1945. SAS & SBS.
Air Commandos, Royal Marine Commandos
3rd British Division 1809-1980. The Iron Division / 3rd (United Kingdom) Division
The British Commonwealth Armed Forces
2nd Canadian Infantry Division, Dieppe "Operation Jubilee" 19th August 1942
Normandy Campaign 6th June – 20th August 1944. Normandy Veterans
Dunkirk Veterans

The Burma Star Association
The Association of WRENS
Royal Marines
Parachute Regiment Association
RAF Bomber Command
Women's Auxiliary Air Force Association
Brigade of Gurkhas.
Submariners Association
The Suez Veterans Association 1945-1956
Royal Lincolnshire Regiment, Egypt
Royal Electrical and Mechanical Engineers Association
Eighth Army, El-Alamein 1942
Italy and Sicily - Anzio 1943 and Casino 1944
Royal Army Medical Corps.
Those who died in the Falklands War 1982
The Grenadier Guards
Fleet Air Arm
Royal Observer Corps Seaborn Wing. Normandy. June to August 1944
Cyprus Veterans' Association 1955-1958
Polish Armed Forces and Civilians in World War Two
Arctic Convoys of the Merchant Navy and Royal Navy (Escorts) in the 78 convoys to Russia
In Memory of Boston Civilians who lost their lives through enemy air raids in two World Wars. RIP
Battle of Jutland. 31st May & 1st June 1916
Gallipoli Campaign 1914-1916
Battle of Amiens 1918, Allied Forces
Battle of the Somme. July 1916-November 1916, British & Commonwealth Casualties

"Greater love hath no man than he lay down his life for his friends"

It was in 2005 that Frank Thompson, a veteran of the war in Korea, approached Boston Borough Council for permission to erect memorial stones in the gardens. Together with his neighbour Les Budding, a Normandy, Dunkirk and Royal Navy veteran, they worked as volunteers to encourage additional memorial plaques to be erected. Today there are 56, complete with wreaths and crosses in place.

The annual cost of maintenance is around £2000, which comes from voluntary donations, due to the generosity of the public, particularly customers of ASDA when there is a collection stall in the entrance to the supermarket. The various Regiments contribute to the cost of their plaques. Boston Borough Council maintains the lawns, flower beds, trees, fencings, pavings and the monument, whilst the "Boston Memorial Plaques Committee" maintains the memorial stones.

The only two remaining committee members, Frank Thompson and Les Budding, now do all the work, and they are looking for volunteers to help them.

Frank Thompson is a born and bred Bostonian, local footballer and cricketer, being one of the founder members of Boston Town Youth Cricket Club in the 1950's. Following National Service in the Royal Leicestershire Regiment, he went on to serve with the Royal Lincolnshire Regiment for 16 years as a WO2 - then he worked as manager with E C Stanwell's, and Taylor's Garages.

Les Budding and Frank Thompson

The present War Memorial

On Armistice Day, 11th November, 2014, the people of Boston were silent in remembrance of all those who have lost their lives in conflicts around the world.

But in particular, a service conducted by the Vicar of St. Botolph's Church, the Reverend Alyson Buxton, was held to dedicate a new memorial commemorating the 100th[h] anniversary of the outbreak of the First World War. The polished granite memorial has been funded entirely by public donations and is dedicated to the 627 men and women from Boston Borough who were casualties in that war. The names were on display at the unveiling by the Mayor of Boston, Cllr. Alison Austin, along with the names of all the donors. Long Sutton stonemason Richard King waived his fee for his expertise in making the monument, only charging for the materials. The reverse face has been left blank, to be engraved in four years' time to mark the centenary of the end of the First World War.

24 Wide Bargate
Pygott and Crone

Estate agents.

The Georgian house of Samuel Henry Jebb, solicitor, and then Joseph Wren, a prosperous corn merchant.

In 1909-1931, this was described as a private residence, believed to be the home of George Holland, of Holland Brothers, the motor trade family, with domestic yard and garden, together with land in the rear and fronting Tawney Street upon which is erected a range of engineering workshops, motor garages, car stores yard and sheds, valued at £5200. Other additions included two Large Sheds and 14 lock-up sheds or garages.
The Freehold Shop and Offices at 26 Wide Bargate with showroom, store room and cycle repairing shop was valued at £1400.

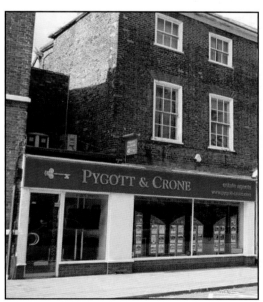

24 Wide Bargate - Pygott and Crone

Another Boston family business was located here in the 1950s, Budge & Mableson, electrical and refrigeration engineers for house, commerce and agriculture, and retailers, before moving across the road to 39 Wide Bargate.
Among others they were followed by Allen's radio and television, also at 61, High Street; also Prime Print.
The first and second floors were occupied by Cooke – Yarborough, Swann and Cockerill, solicitors, and agents for Prudential Insurance and Nottingham Building Society.

26 Wide Bargate
Newton Fallowell

*Region Chain of Estate Agents owned by
Mark Newton.*

Throughout the 20th Century this has been the offices
of an estate agent.

Newton Fallowell

In the early years it was Simons Ingamells and Young, then Simons & Ingamells, then Simons & Co., Who sold out to Halifax Estate Agents, who in turn were bought by James Eley & Son, which remained trading under that name until recent years when it was taken over by Newton Fallowell.

'Simons' and 'Eleys' were traditional Chartered Surveyors and Auctioneers serving the entire property market, whereas Halifax and Newton Fallowell concentrated only on house sales.

26A Wide Bargate
Heron Foods

Frozen foods retail. National company.

Over 150 years ago, William Holmes Holland was a large scale farmer and miller in Butterwick. Married to Ann Calthrop, they had 13 children. George and Charles Holland left their farming family in native Butterwick to serve apprenticeships in Boston with William Barton, who had bought an ironmongery business at 24 Strait Bargate, this business having been founded by Charles Fendelow in about 1840. This is the shop next to what is now QD Stores.

26A Wide Bargate - Heron Foods

The brothers were among the youngest of those 13 children, and there was no work for them on the family farm (farming was having a bad time in the severe agricultural depression of the 1840s). Ultimately, Mr. Barton died, and the Holland Brothers bought the business from his widow, Sarah Ann Barton. That was the beginning of what became the well-known Holland Brothers family business in Lincolnshire.

Charles, the youngest brother, was a keen cyclist, and he became champion of the Boston Bicycle Club in 1878 riding a Penny Farthing, examples of which were still in the company's possession until the 1990s. As a result of this interest, components were made up and sold as "Holland Cycles", a diversification from ironmongery which in the years ahead was to be very successful. There is still a "Holland Cycle" on display at the Lincolnshire Life Museum.

Ladies 'Sit Up and Beg' Cycle advert

In 1901, this Ladies 'Sit Up and Beg' Cycle was priced from 8 guineas to 12 guineas, and for an extra guinea you could also have a free wheel and a brake!

At the turn of the century, motor repairs and sales began to find a place in the business and recognising the potential of the "new invention" they decided to concentrate on this, and accordingly sold the ironmongery business for £5000 to the Hutson Brothers, who continued to trade at 24 Strait Bargate, until moving to 11 Wide Bargate.

Hollands bought 26A, Wide Bargate, and continued to carry on their cycle and motor dealers business at "Boston Popular Wheel". Charles Holland lived at No. 24 Wide Bargate.

It was always said that Charles Holland was the first man in Boston to own and drive a car. It was a Humber 2 Seater (one seat situated behind the other) which had a maximum speed of 20mph, but the speed limit was only 12mph.

As the years went by, the bicycle trade contracted and the motor business expanded and prospered. In 1901 Charles' son, Robert, was apprenticed to the Wolseley Company in Birmingham, and for a time worked with Herbert Austin, founder of the Austin Motor Company, who was then in the drawing office.

In 1903, the company began selling imported Peugeot cars, which were to be the forerunner of popular motoring, and one of the firm's sales can still be seen in the Science Museum to this day.

In 1905, Charles, by now an enthusiastic driver, was given a medal by the Lincolnshire Automobile Club for the substantial feat of driving 100 miles non-stop.

Holland Bros. Ltd. Advertisement from the turn of the century

The business became a limited company in 1920, and three years later, the company relinquished its Ford dealership which they had held for some years, and became Morris Distributors. In 1927 the Bargate Showrooms at 26a Wide Bargate were extensively modernised and further developments took place when the coach builders business in Tawney Street was acquired from Mr. Walter Jones. Even some ancient ponds, remaining from the days of Tunnard's Deer Park, had to be filled in before building works could commence.

In 1941, the Bargate Showrooms and stores were severely damaged by German bombs and it was not until 1952 that they were finally rebuilt.

In the 1970's there were tremendous changes within the business, a new commercial workshops were built in 1972 with other substantial alterations made in Tawney Street. In 1976 the company bought the entire share capital of R. M. Wright (Boston) Ltd., the Austin distributors for South Lincolnshire, their premises being further down Wide Bargate, and the operations were entirely absorbed into the parent company.
The family owned motor company then acted as distributors for virtually the whole range of Leyland vehicles, Leyland parts wholesalers, and built commercial vehicle bodies. In fact it was one the most comprehensive garages in the county, with branches in Sleaford (1901-1989), Spalding (1938-1989) and Skegness (1971-1995).

In 1984 the Bargate showroom was leased to Wilkinson's Hardware Stores, who subsequently sub-leased to Heron Frozen Foods, when they moved to Pescod Square shopping centre.

The main showroom moved to the old R. M. Wright premises on the corner of Tawney Street and Wide Bargate, and in 1989 that was sold, to be redeveloped for Iceland Frozen Foods. A major redevelopment of the garage site behind Bargate, with frontage to Tawney Street was carried out, including the installation of self-service petrol pumps on the forecourt, new car spray workshop and parts department.

Four generations of the Holland family from the original George and Charles successfully managed and expanded this motor trade business from its Boston base.

Branches in Sleaford (1901), Spalding (1938), Central Garage, Skegness (1971) were added. And in 1976, Hollands purchased the business of R. M. Wright at No.38, Wide Bargate (now Iceland).

They were main dealers and distributors for Morris, Austin, Jaguar, BMC, Rootes Group, Triumph, and major participants in the Retail Motor Association representing the interests of motor dealers throughout the UK.

Finally, in 1995, the current generation of Holland Brothers sold the business and remaining premises to The Lincolnshire Co-Operative Group, who at that time were expanding their motor trade interests.

The Co-Op has since carried out redevelopment schemes including the Doctors' surgery, Co-Op pharmacy, and Robin Hood car park.

More recently, the Co-Op have submitted a planning application for the car park to be redeveloped into a Lidl Supermarket.

28 Wide Bargate - Chattertons Solicitors

28 Wide Bargate
Chattertons Solicitors
Solicitors with Offices across Lincolnshire
Senior Partner: Peter Lawson

It was in 1972 that Frank Cammack opened the Boston office of Chattertons Solicitors at 16B Main Ridge.

He was joined by Peter Lawson, and in 1978 Chattertons merged with Millington Simpsons and Giles (Partners were Dick Giles, son of Sir Oswald Giles, and John Philpott) moving into their Wide Bargate premises, and retaining staff members including Bill Barrand, Sid Woods, Tom Povey and Arthur Oughton.

Ever increasing expansion of the business necessitated additional first floor offices in New Street, which in 1992 moved to South Square.

Senior partners of Chattertons at Boston have been Frank Cammack, Peter Cropley and Peter Lawson, and additional Partners have included Stuart Cox, Elizabeth Hopkins, Katherine Bunting, Edward Conway, and Robert Smith.

This building has been a solicitor's office since at least 1868, when Simpson and Millington were in practice. Previous senior partners include Sir Oswald B. Giles DL, and his son O.R. (Dick) Giles, DL, both of whom were Deputy Lieutenants of Lincolnshire.

Over the years, Chattertons has expanded by incorporating additional private practices, and is now represented not only in Boston, but also in Grantham, Horncastle, Lincoln, Newark, Sleaford, Spalding and Stamford by some 29 Partners, and 200 staff.

Opposite here is Bargate Green

Wide Bargate was originally two lanes of highway, with a green between them and a few buildings.
In previous times Bargate Green was rough green area with the two Russian cannons and a German tank on display.
With the exception of Wednesdays, this is now a public 'Pay and Display' car park, owned by the Borough Council. However, it is perhaps known best as part of Boston Market, for every Wednesday it is transformed into one of the UK's largest open air markets, filled with market stalls, and the famous weekly auction which has been a feature of Boston since time immemorial.

Russian cannons on Bargate Green

For centuries, dating back to the 12th Century, "The Green" has been devoted to selling all manner of goods by public auction. These days it is recognised as a prime tourist attraction, bringing visitors from all over the country, especially the Midlands, by car and coach. The well-known auctioneering firms from the past have included Killingworth and Dunn (Jack Killingworth, Herbert Woods, Don Holmes), Mackinder, Bennett and Balderston; Thos. Balderston and Co. (Tom and Tim Balderston), and James Eley & Son (Jim and Bruce Mather, and Dudley Bryant). Ian Naylor followed, now it is L&B Auctions.

A view of Bargate Green

Balderston's were originally from Spilsby; Edgar, Brundle (Brun) and Thomas (Tom) Balderston. After leaving the RAF in 1947, Tom opened a small office in Grants Lane, expanding into 24 Market Place. As Auctioneers they were involved in the Cattle Market and the Bargate Green auctions, and operated on the Green from 1947 to 1990, when James Eley and Son took over their pitch to add to their own next door.

This auction is well-known far and wide for selling produce, plants, shrubs, bric-a-brac, memorabilia, garden equipment, motor cars, motor bikes, cycles, timber. In fact, "anything dead"!!

The ancient auction rules of "Caveat Emptor", ("buyer beware"), "sold as seen", "Let your eye be your guide, and your pocket be your judge" still apply - albeit now tempered by the inevitable modern "Mr. Health & Safety"!

Thousands of people will remember Dudley Bryant being a fixture every Wednesday with his auctioneer's bell and stick, selling plants, produce, motor cars and bikes, cycles, household goods, seed potatoes, farm and garden equipment, etc, even on one occasion, a barrel organ, complete with its live monkey. 'You name it, Dudley would sell it!'

Don't "nod" your head at Dudley while he is in selling mode! It costs you money! I remember well, one Wednesday when I visited the Green, and spotted a big crowd around him. As he looked across at me, I nodded and said *"Good Morning"*. Immediately, he brought down the hammer, and said *"Sold"*. I had bought a lovely bunch of flowers, which Dudley told me to give to my wife as a surprise!!

Dudley Bryant, with porter, Liz on the Bargate Green

Boston is famous for its open-air markets. For hundreds of years, countless stall holders have offered goods for sale. It is the largest market in Lincolnshire.

Boston Market has a long history, from way back in the 1400's at the time of Boston May Fair, there was prize fighting, bull baiting, and the beast mart. The only revolting spectacle in the fair was the common exposure and sale of slaves, or villeins as they were called. These unfortunate individuals were arranged, like a beast in a stall, just outside the Bar-gate, each one having an iron collar around his neck with his name and that of his owner. The price of an ordinary slave was 13 shillings and four pence and in the days before divorce became easily available, it was also not uncommon for a man to put a halter around his wife's neck, and sell her for half a crown.

In 1938, The Green and the Auction Market were described as "Without its Wednesday market Boston would lose half its attractiveness. Even early on a Wednesday morning there is an atmosphere that makes it different from the ordinary day. The town puffs its chest out and feels more important because of all the bustling activity. Plank-laden carts discharge their cargo for deft hands to set up the stalls. Lorries with beast or poultry rattle down the streets, farmers and merchants drive up in their cars, and buses from the country districts bring visitors.

Wednesday Market on the 'Green'

The 'Green' always popular with locals and tourists

Down at the cattle pens they were already selling beast and I stood for a moment by the ring. But that is only one side of the market, and to the non-farmer the least interesting.

Only a few yards away the casual spectator can find much more to attract his attention. Any Wednesday on Bargate Green you can walk around to find "lots" so strangely assorted that you fancy no one will ever buy them, but they do. Here is a great battery of cycles, sacks of potatoes are grouped a yard or two away and chairs, soon to be sold, are used by jaded auction attenders, a trunk load of books, a mass of twisted iron, a Chinese picture and planks of timber.

What's that he's saying now? *"How much for Nelly?"* Is this a slave market? But the assistant is holding up a dog. *"Now come along, how much for Nelly? He's a grand dog. A shilling sir? Oh, come along, be serious, there's a collar and lead worth more than that. He's a fine ratter too, is Nelly. How much am I offered? Is that the only offer I have? Very well, it's going for a shilling. A shilling to this gentleman."*

A few of the buyers detach themselves from the edge of the crowd, and move over to a young man whose hands are never still, and he talks all the time. At his feet are pieces of brass, copper, taps and knobs, and he is demonstrating and selling polish with which to clean them, at sixpence a bottle.

Two gentlemen are selling razor blades, and point out that *"it's silly to go paying high prices when you can get them of just the same quality at one third of the price".".*

So, apart from the selling of animals, which ended years ago, not much has changed over the last century, and Bargate Green continues to attract both local residents, and large numbers of visitors from all over the country.

Today, the Market Stalls on Bargate Green regularly include:

Helen Jacklin, from Gainsborough.
She started on Bargate Green one year ago, adding to her stalls in Gainsborough, Newark, and Hemswell, selling hosiery, specialising in socks and underwear. She finds Boston people very friendly.

Jehovah's Witnesses
This stall distributes religious literature free of charge to anyone interested in the Holy Bible

Steve McDonald
Mr. McDonald is a Bostonian, an Old Boy of Kitwood Boys' School. He has been a regular on the market for 15 years, selling hardware and household merchandise, but specialising in gloves. The summer months are best for business, when his best customers are the tourists, especially holidaymakers from Skegness.

Philip Norman and his daughter, Maria.

Mr. Norman is a retired engineer from Peterborough. They started on the market in October 2014, selling silver jewellery, and ladies hairbands made by Maria. He says his only claim to fame is that he helped to build the Jubilee Line Underground Railway in London in the early 1970's. He feels there is a business waiting out there to be developed, and that it could be in franchising.

Walton Meadows

Coming from Chapel St. Leonards he started on the market at the end of October 2014. There has also been a shop in Chapel for 10 years, and another one in Skegness for one year, selling the full range of fishing tackle.

Magpie Nest

Proprietor, Des Ellerby is a Bostonian selling collectables and antiques. He started attending the Green on Wednesdays in June 2014, and has seen business improving in that time. He also has market stalls in Newark (Mondays); Horncastle (Thursdays); Louth (Fridays); Grantham (Saturdays).

John Young

Coming from Addlethorpe, he has been standing on Boston Market for 15 years, and had a regular pitch in the Market Place on Wednesdays and Saturdays. When the recent refurbishment of the Market Place was in progress, he, like all the other stallholders, transferred to Wide Bargate and the Green. On completion of the works, the stalls went back into the Market Place, but unfortunately there was not a big enough stall space available for him to return to his pitch, so he was forced to stay on Bargate Green, and only now comes to Boston on Wednesdays. He sells a full range of ladies' and gents footwear, and still hopes to get a big enough pitch in the Market Place.

Malc Haw

Mr. Haw originates from North Yorkshire, but moved to Skegness 18 years ago, and been a regular on Bargate Green for five years.
He sells genuine military surplus stocks of clothing, footwear, etc. British, German, French, Austrian, Belgian and Dutch.
He is a regular, come rain or shine – he is always there.

Mal Haw

Pete's Outlet

Peter Johns comes from Nottingham, and has been a regular now for three years. He sells sweets and cakes, and also has stalls at Ingoldmells (Saturdays) and Billinghay (Sundays).

Chris Thomas and Son

Father and Son operating the well-known fruit and vegetable stall next to the Auction site. Chris has been coming to the Green from Nottingham since 2009. A regular Market Trader with stands at Melton Mowbray (Sundays and Tuesdays); Allington, Derbyshire (Fridays); Willington (Saturdays).

Fat Jack's Catering Trailer

Proprietor, Mr. Malc Haw, with manageress Natalie Sherburn. Opened this new modern facility in February 2015. There is a varied menu of food and drinks on offer to traders and the public, including hot soups, full English breakfast, burgers, crisps, and sausage and bacon baps.

Chris Thomas & Son

The replica Stocks on the Bargate Green

The Stocks

The original, early 19th century stocks fell into disrepair, and were removed in the 1950's. Today's 1990's replica, are still there as a reminder to petty criminals of serious punishment for such wrong doers, but no longer in use! The originals were located in the north east corner of the Market Place, and later were put on display at the Guildhall Museum.

The last two people to be locked in the stocks were Barber Joe and Squeely Green.

Squeely Green was a strange fellow. He and his wife used to bury the stray cats and dogs for the Corporation. But after the event he would go with a rake and dig the animals up again, which meant they had to be buried once more, which meant he got double fees!!

Barber Joe was the last person to be put in the stocks. He used to go in the Angel Inn and shave the countrymen. He would take his shaving tin in his pocket, and put it in the Tap Room fire to boil and when the water was hot, got down to business. He did well, but was not satisfied, so he also set up at the White Hart on Sundays. This angered the other barbers and they complained. So Joe was put in the stocks by Constables Jim Maline and Joe Ashton.

30 Wide Bargate
Cammack & Sons Ltd

Family business of furniture and interior furnishings retailers.

One family running the same business in Boston for 95 years and a business originally founded 158 years ago.

The Cammack family goes back to the 18th century in Benington and Boston.

Francis Alfred Cammack founded Cammacks in 1919, following demobilisation from the RAF in World War One. He was a cabinet maker at 56 Wide Bargate, having been an apprentice to J. H. Small in the Market Place.

Cammack & Sons Ltd

In 1931 his three sons (Ken, Frank & Sydney) worked with him, although Father was very much in charge, and he sold No. 50 to Edward White, purchasing the business of Hill and Sons at 30 Wide Bargate who were Antique Dealers, Undertakers, Upholsterers. That business was originally founded by John Hill in 1856 at Red Lion Street, and in 1888 he bought John Kennington's business at this site. They were specialists in restoration of Jacobean, Queen Anne, Chippendale and Sheraton furniture. They were also furniture manufacturers.

The site was redeveloped, and the present 4 storey shop built, an early example of a steel girdered building, with oil fired heating and included Boston's first motorised lift. It was described as "one of the finest stores seen in Boston at the time".

It is interesting to note that the site of this shop was part of Tunnard's Deer Park belonging to No. 20 Wide Bargate.

During World War Two all three sons served in the Armed Forces, whilst Elsie Cammack (wife of Sydney, and mother of John Cammack) carried on the business.

Further expansion included the purchase of Webster's Gun Shop at No. 30A
The 3rd generation of Cammack's, John and Roger continued the business, and now the 4th generation, Tony and Richard, sons of Roger and John, now carry on the tradition in modern times.

During the Second World War, a 250kg bomb fell in front of Cammack' shop on Good Friday 1940. It took several days to get it out, like other bombs which fell in the Boston area. The land on which Boston is built meant that bombs went deeper and deeper into the silt as digging progressed.

On another German raid a bomb fell in West Street hitting The Royal George pub and Loveley's bakers. Two well- known teenagers, Kathleen and Audrey Loveley lost their lies. Also killed was John Faulkner, and a soldier's wife Nancy Harris and her three children.

A more detailed story of air raids on Boston during the Second World War can be found in the book *"Boston at War"* written by the well-known Boston historian and author, Martin Middlebrook, from where the Cammack's story was taken.

Good Friday 1940, a 250Kg bomb fell in front of Cammack's

Metal plate set in the pavement outside Cammack's shop

It was at this point in Bargate that there was a turnpike or toll bar. Presumably this is how Bargate got its name. There is a metal plate, possibly unique, set in the pavement outside Cammack's shop which marks the spot. Where there was a gate across Bargate and which a toll was paid for all cattle to enter Boston.

Toll fees used to pay for road maintenance from Boston to Spilsby via Hilldyke.

30A Wide Bargate

In the 1920's to 1960's this was a separate shop occupied by John Thomas Gray, fishmonger; William Henry Stanwell, butcher; Webster's, gunsmiths and sports outfitters; Norman Throp Ltd., radio and TV.

Then in 1966 it was incorporated into Cammack's Furniture store.

32A Wide Bargate
Wilcox & Carter
Family Jewellers'.

Current proprietors are Mr Noel Gleeson and Mrs Kathleen Gleeson.

Original occupier Mr Wilcox (originally 'Wilcosh') was a Polish commando in service in the Second World War and was seriously wounded in action, the injuries which resulted in him losing a leg.

Leaving the Forces he was sent to Scotland for retraining as a watch repairer and came to Boston to work for Stanley Hopper at Hoppers the Jewellers in Strait Bargate.

32A Wide Bargate Wilcox & Carter and 32 Wide Bargate Studio Metamorphosis

While working there he met Sidney Carter, from Coventry, and eventually they set up the partnership of Wilcox and Carter in 1959.

On retirement the business was purchased by Noel and Kathleen Gleeson from Derby, who continue to provide a first class service today.

Before the Second World War the premises were Louth Dyeworks and Steam Laundry Company.

32 Wide Bargate
Studio Metamorphosis

Hair and Beauty salon, Skin and laser centre, opened May 2012.

One of the oldest established firms of auctioneers and estate agents was established in Market Place in about 1880 by Ben Killingworth, who brought into partnership Mr. Dunn, the firm being known as Killingworth and Dunn, moving here in 1933. Later, Jack Killingworth, the youngest student ever to qualify as a Fellow of the Auctioneers Institute, inherited the business, renaming it J. A. Killingworth and bringing in a partner, Herbert Woods. After the death of Jack Killingworth, Don Holmes joined the firm from Tateson's of Spalding in 1968.

Don reminds us that as well as the business of estate agency, surveyors and valuers, Killingworth's were renowned auctioneers operating a chicken auction in South Square, Boston, (the chickens used to arrive by ferry), and later on Bargate Green, and at the Poultry Market (now a car park adjacent to the New England Hotel in Wide Bargate). Chickens were held in fixed pens. Fresh produce and game was also auctioned every Wednesday on Market Day.

Killingworth's also operated the cattle, pig and sheep auction, specialising in the sale of pigs from fixed iron pens on the Cattle Market and Bargate Green.

Killingworth's sold out to Earl & Lawrence, based at Sleaford, and then it later became Haart Estate Agents.

Don Holmes

34-36 Wide Bargate - Coneys

34-36 Wide Bargate & 2A Tawney Street
Coneys (Coneys Tailors Ltd)

Mens' and Ladies' outfitters,

The business originated in Boston in the 1930's at No. 1, Wide Bargate (now Santander Bank) and moved to its present location in 1956 and a number of small adjacent shops were bought by the late Mr Alec Coney, a notable farmer and businessman, as and when they became available.

Among them, a china shop, a tobacconist, and sweet shop. The china shop was owned by Maltbys, who then went into business selling cars in Horncastle Road. They acquired the Mercedes franchise, and are now based on the Boardsides.

Coneys is a long established and respected business name in the County. They started in Alford in 1856, and as time went by had as many as 11 tailor's shops in Lincolnshire and adjacent counties, later on moving into farming.

2A Tawney Street

A Ladies' department was added to the Men's shop in Bargate in the 1960's. In 1986 the adjoining premises in Tawney Street, which had been a sub fire station, and then Fyffes banana warehouse was acquired, and the Ladies Department was enlarged. Downstairs in the ex-banana warehouse, a boutique called "Alix" was added but later it was moved upstairs, and replaced by the coffee shop downstairs. The bottom floor was rented to Stan and Kay Brockbanks who operated their business Pilgrim Decor, and the coffee shop. There followed a number of short term occupiers of the downstairs premises, such as Lillo's restaurant, De Niro's restaurant, and now Niko's restaurant.

Coneys Tailor's business was sold to Mr. Scott Crowson in October 2009, but the premises is still owned by the Coney family, along with Nos. 30 and 32. Mrs. Gillian Brown, Mr. Alec Coney's daughter still controls the premises. The store is managed by Mr. Philip Curtis.

Round the corner on Tawney Street was a tobacconist's kiosk.

Before Coneys occupied the present premises, there had been several small shops along the frontage now forming Coney's, and included:-

Misses M & G Day, florists; Eric Winfield, electrical engineer; G. Livermore, confectioner (back entrance); J. Baumber, sweets and tobacconist; M. Jessop, embroidery and wools; Trentstreet Factors Ltd., wireless factors; Hall & Son, Saddlers; H Middlebrook, potato merchant; The Bargate China Company; Misses G & E Cobb.

Iceland Frozen Foods

Here is Tawney Street

Wide Bargate
Iceland Frozen Foods
National freezer and frozen foods retailer.

The history of these premises was connected to road transport and engineering for nearly 150 years.

From 1830 coach makers and wheelwrights Ablewhite and Brough, then in 1855 this was Woollard and Son, carriage works and coach makers.

In the 1930's it was T. Rickard and Sons Ltd. Agricultural Implement Agents, followed by Stocks (1920) Ltd. (Motors), motor engineers, who were incorporated into R. M. Wright Ltd., during the 1950's and 60's and then finally taken over by Holland Bros. Ltd. to add to their operations in Tawney Street and Sleaford.

40 Wide Bargate
Departure Lounge Travel
Travel Agents.

Departure Lounge was established in December 2009, arising out of the closure of Stephen Walker Travel in the Market Place. The staff recognised that they had over 70 years' experience in the travel industry, so three Bostonians, Jenny Robson, Debbie King and Annette Whiting, with the help of Jenny's husband, Tim Robson, decided to continue offering travel services to the people of Boston and district.

40 Wide Bargate - Departure Lounge Travel and 42 Wide Bargate - DPS, Digital Printing and Copy Services

They have built an enviable reputation as an independent, solely owned travel advisor offering high quality and personal service, selling all types of travel from once in a lifetime round the world tours, cruising, rail travel, trips to the theatre, or coach travel to London, covering all age groups. The company is ABTA bonded and members of the Elite Travel Group.

Prior to Departure Lounge the premises were occupied by Newton Fallowell, estate agents.

Jenny has many recollections of the premises being occupied by many different types of business - for example, Lodge Sports, Top Drawer ladies' fashion, Four Seasons guest house, a restaurant, and her mother and father remember back in the 1950s it was occupied by a grocers called Mark Baker.

42 Wide Bargate

DPS, Digital Printing and Copy Services

Printing and photocopying.

In earlier times this has been Moses Fruit and Veg Shop; Lodge Sports, owned by Peter Gedney; Prime Print.

40 and 42 Wide Bargate

This was a single property owned by Mark Baker, grocer and provision merchant in the 1930s to 1960s. The shop was always pervaded by the delicious smell of freshly roasted and ground coffee.

I was privileged to be invited by Colin and Janet Pape to their lovely home to talk about 42 Wide Bargate, and Mark Baker Ltd, in particular.

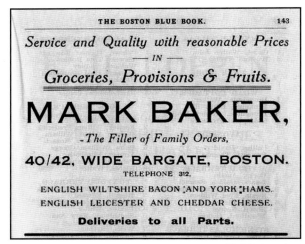

Mark Baker advert

Janet worked as a shop assistant in the grocery and provisions shop for 10 years from 1956 to 1966. She spoke fondly of her time there, and of Mr. Mark Baker in particular. She remembers him as a quiet gentleman who treated his staff as an extension of his family. He was also very artistic and designed the labels and price tickets for the goods on sale.

He had two senior assistants, the formidable Miss Doris Semper, and Stan Chote who looked after the bacon and provisions. There were 11 staff members, and each had to display competence in product knowledge, price calculation and customer service. Mark Baker provided a delivery service - first with two bicycle delivery boys and later with a van delivery service. Provision products such as butter, cheese, lard, and bacon were purchased in bulk. The staff would then break them down into smaller quantities, wrap, weigh and price them, whether it was coffee from Brazil or Costa Rica, tea from India or Ceylon, Danish butter, bacon or cheese, or products from Australia, New Zealand, South Africa or Cyprus. A pleasant extra for customers and passers-by was the ever present aroma of freshly ground roasted coffee.

Mark Baker had a wide range of customers, but the bulk of the trade was with the Boston business families, and the farming families.

Janet rattled off names such as the Johnsons, Taits, Hollands, Towells, Cammacks, Enderbys, etc., etc.

The business ceased trading in the late 1960s due chiefly to the lack of parking facilities, the advent of the big self-service supermarkets, which offered plenty of free parking facilities, and cut pricing, etc.

Janet and Colin are both proud of their Boston and district origins. Janet was born and brought up in Hartley Street and Colin haled from Thorpe St. Peter near Wainfleet.

Colin, who is the present principal of H. H. Adkins (Contractors) Ltd., the local builders based in Wyberton West Road, says that he started his own business as a Quantity Surveyor in 1953, in offices on top of Avril's hairdressing salon at 35 Wide Bargate. He is still very much hands on, and puts in a full day at the office.

Top Drawer, Margaret Jessop, H. L. Berry

Janet and Colin gave me a brief tour of their charming home, during which I found we had two things in common. We came from musical families, and were brought up as Wesleyan Methodists. Janet and Colin worship at the Centenary Wesleyan Methodist Church in Red Lion Street.

I saw Janet's grand piano, and hoped she was going to play one or two of Charles Wesley's hymns and that I might break into song. She did not. My singing would have spoilt what was a pleasant afternoon's visit.

These premises later this became Top Drawer, ladies' fashion Shop owned by John Leake, with his wife and daughter, until they sold the business to Mr. John Woodward of Fantasy Island, at Ingoldmells, when it was renamed The Four Seasons House of Fashion. It then became the Four Seasons Restaurant offering Bed and Breakfast upstairs, until the premises were divide into two separate units as Nos. 40 and 42.

44-46 Wide Bargate
'One Stop' Convenience Store
Formerly, Mills CTN, Mills Group Ltd, national convenience retail store, who purchased it from Berry's newsagents.

This was originally two individual shops.

44 Wide Bargate

A mixture of watch and clock makers, drapers and butchers and later occupiers have included Elizabeth Mary Goose, ladies' outfitter; Madge Major, ladies' outfitter and Major School of Motoring; Margaret Jessop, wool shop; Pips and Petals took this shop in mid-1980's, opening up as a flower shop, but when Asda opened nearby they took all the trade, and the shop was changed to needlework, and then ultimately sold to Mills Newsagents to become part of the enlarged premises.

46 Wide Bargate

From about 1840 this was owned by William Gale from Sussex, hairdresser, perfumer and tobacconist; then in 1896, Harry James Maddison, from 51 Pen Street established his hairdressers, newsagents and tobacconist business. In 1921, Ellen Mary Maddison took over the business on the death of her husband. In 1961 the hairdressing side of the business was given up, with the remainder continuing until 1967 when Ellen Mary and her daughter May Maddison retired, the business being sold to H. L. Berry, newsagents, also at 28 Horncastle Road and 108 Fydell Street. Ten years later, Mills newsagents took over, and they incorporated No. 44 next door to create a larger shop, until 2012 when the present occupiers, "One Stop" took over.

One Stop

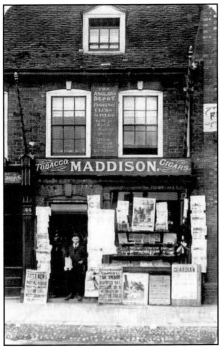

Maddison's

Maddison's paper round covering Bargate, Hartley Street, Tawney Street, Willoughby Road, Spilsby Road, and Tower Road used to take one hour to deliver every morning starting at 6.30am, and for over 23 years it was done by Mrs. D. Pogson and 11 of her children. The paper round came into the family from her brother, and she handed it down to her daughter, and then to her brother who later became a Metropolitan Police sergeant in Romford.

In 1924 Mr, Eric Lammie started his hairdressing apprenticeship, when haircuts (a short back and sides) cost 4d and a shave was 2d and 6d for a shampoo. His wages were five shillings a week and he worked at Maddison's until 1961, when he left to set up his own business at Bargate Bridge where he worked until retiring in 1984, aged 74. By then he was doing Beatle haircuts, the "Boston", and "rat's tail". By the time of his retirement, he had cut the hair of five generations of two local families, Cammacks and Hutsons. He was the only Boston hairdresser to have been East Midlands Area President of the National Hairdressers' Federation. His business was taken over by Mr. Sid Bolland of Main Ridge.

48 Wide Bargate

Red Cow Hotel
Public House.

Built in the mid-18th century, this Grade II Listed Building, has always been a pub. Indeed it was one of the most popular market pubs in the heyday of Boston Cattle Market, where all the cattle dealers would 'refresh themselves', particularly as this market pub which was allowed to stay open until 4pm on market days, instead of the usual 2pm closing time which applied to the other town pubs.

48 Wide Bargate - Red Cow Hotel

Landlords have included Horry (1851); James Eley (1882); Fred Dolton (1896); Arthur Simmons, Harold Rayson, Phil Harris, Trevor Walker. In 2013 the hotel was purchased by Ikram Qutab, the licensee being Muhammed Qutab of Drinks and Dine Ltd.

Travel in Boston in the 1700's was something of an adventure, mostly being done on horseback.
For longer distances, there was the stage coach which ran between London and York, stopping at Stamford and Grantham on the old Great North Road, now the A1(M).

Then in 1786, a new stage coach which carried four passengers, began a three times per week service from Spilsby, Boston, Spalding, Peterborough and Huntingdon to London, and returning the next morning at 5am. These coaches stopped off at the Red Cow, Red Lion, and Peacock Inns in Boston.

Have you noticed the Boston Borough's Three Crowns plaque on the gate post?

In 1972, Phil Harris, having served in the British Foreign Service, asked himself *"What does a retired diplomat then do for a living?"*

He contacted Watneys Brewery and applied to take over the Red Cow, becoming a most successful and popular "mine host" from 1972 to 1980.

At that time the Cattle Market was still operating, and many well known cattle dealers frequented the Red Cow every Wednesday including Frans Buitelaar, "Uncle Ben" Newton, Billy Marsden from Sheffield, Les Dion, Watson the Freiston butcher.

Average bar takings were £30 per day (double that amount on Wednesdays). Watneys Red Barrel was the beer to drink and in 1972 beer was 12.5 pence per pint !!

In 1980, Phil retired again, this time to run the Causeway Guest House at Wyberton. In 2005, he became managing director, and is now the President of Boston and County Club.

There were also several businesses operating from The Red Cow Yard which included from time to time, Baker and Soars, builders and plumbers; W. Wells and Son, tarpaulin manufacturers. Killingworth and Dunn, auctioneers operated the weekly chicken and poultry market from this rear yard, moving to the Poultry Market next to the New England Hotel.

In 1882, James Eley started his auctioneering career in the Red Cow Yard.

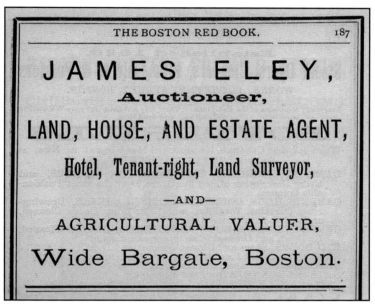

James Eley advert

During the Second World War, the Red Cow was a favourite watering hole for the airmen from RAF Coningsby, and Dudley Bryant recalls his Latin master at Stamford School, Mr. A H (Tony) Tomlin, who used to visit the pub when on leave. He served with RAF Bomber Command. At school on rare occasions, he would reminisce about some of his wartime experiences, particularly when Dudley told him that he knew the Red Cow.

Tony Tomlin served with distinction as a Lancaster pilot in 617 Squadron, and was awarded the DFC and Bar as well as an AFC. A man of great courage, but also one who modestly understated his achievements, he had two crash landings in a three week period during bombing raids on Berlin in 1943. His aircraft was badly hit by a night fighter and a starboard engine caught fire. As captain he made the decision to carry on, drop his bombs on Berlin and then fly back to Woodhall Spa on only three engines. While approaching the runway, a port side engine failed as well, and so he landed the aircraft in the dark in a field just short of the landing zone. His seven man crew were unhurt. Courage, indeed.

50-54 Wide Bargate

The Georgians

Private nursing home.

When Anglian Water Authority left Boston, moving its entire administration to Peterborough, these premises were purchased by Garth, Bob and Margaret Isaac. Together with John and Patricia Ball, they set about investing a substantial sum of money to convert this historic and important building into what we all now know as The Georgians Nursing Home. It is the only such nursing home in the town centre, and has built up an enviable reputation as one of the best care homes in the area, benefitting from its central location. In 2014, it was sold to Mr. Kim Patel of Bedford.

The Georgians

This award winning privately owned Care Home accommodates 45 residents.

Maps of 1741 show buildings on this site and this magnificent property with its imposing frontage to Wide Bargate, probably built as three houses in 1760, dominates the nothern end of Bargate. It is a Grade II listed building.

50 Wide Bargate

In 1869 this was purchased from Benjamin Soulby Simpson for £850 by George Wise. Aged just 28 he was an attorney, solicitor and notary public, and lived here with his family and domestic servants.
He became clerk to the local board, charity trustees and to Donington Turnpike Trustees. He sold the house in 1876 to Joseph Lightfoot, farmer from Wood Enderby for £1,150, who stayed until 1892 when John Evelyn Williams is listed as being here. He was civil engineer to Witham General Commissioners and engineer to Witham Outfall Board

From 1905 to 1919 it was the home of Percy E. Wrinch MB, physician and surgeon, who had moved from 19 Wide Bargate. Then it was sold to Dr. Arthur Tuxford of Skirbeck for £1,100 who remained there until his death in 1928. Dr Tuxfords' widow sold the house to Reginald John Manning Moulder, dentist. In 1932, he moved to Holland House, 69, Wide Bargate, across the road, having sold to Witham and Steeping Rivers Catchment Board for £1,400.

By 1953 Lincolnshire River Board had taken over the building, before becoming Anglian Water Authority who remained there until 1986 when it was sold to become The Georgians Nursing Home.

52 Wide Bargate

As with No. 50, this property - which has a familiar historic background - has seen many owners and occupiers.

There is a date of 1786 scratched on stone at the east end of the frontage, just round the corner. In 1805, it was owned by John Broughton, brewer, who was succeeded by Thomas Broughton, porter dealer and tanner, and twice Mayor of Boston in 1928 and 1834. Then in 1849, Charles Dawson, brewer and spirit merchant lived here with his domestic servants until 1863 when it was sold to John Oldrid, and occupied by his son in law Thomas Scrivener with family and servants. The property remained the Scrivener family home for many years until it became the offices of J. & J. Beaulah Ltd. Canners who had also taken over the range of buildings at the rear (No. 54) which had been a brewery, Anderson's Feather Factory and in part, Framlingham and Eastern Counties Co-operative Egg and Poultry Society, egg merchants.

In 1962, this house, which had become offices, was sold to Lincolnshire River Board for £12,000, incorporated Holland County Council Children's Department, becoming Anglian Water Authority in 1986, and in 2000 joining up with No. 50 to become The Georgians.

Boston Shopping Park

Boston Shopping Park

56-60 Wide Bargate
In 2006, Asda moved to a larger site at Sleaford Road and the former supermarket was re-developed into several individual retail units.

W. M. Morrison PLC
National Supermarket, opened in June 2011, who bought out Netto Food Store.

Morrisons, Sports Direct, Home Bargains, Brantano

Sports Direct.Com
Fashion clothing and sports equipment, opened in October 2006.

Home Bargains
National retailer of home wares. Owned by T. J. Morris Ltd., of Liverpool.

Brantano Footwear
National retailer of footwear.

Card Factory
Opened in June 2013 to supplement their shop in Strait Bargate.

Bathstore

T. K. Maxx
International discount retailer of ladies' and mens' clothing, home accessories. Opened in September 2007.

Bathstore
National company specialising in bathroom goods and furniture, opened in September 2006.

Gala Bingo, Boston
National bingo operator, opened in January 2007, occupying the upper floors above the supermarket fronting Wide Bargate.

Gala Bingo

Prior to this site being re-developed, it was a petrol filling station operated by Asda and previously owned by Mr Bill Maltby in conjunction with his adjoining BMW car showroom and workshops.

Before the development of this retail park, this area was dominated by two of the most successful Boston family businesses - J. and J. Beaulah's canning factory and Edward White Ltd.

Edward White Ltd

Ed. White Ltd. was originally established at 70 Wide Bargate, as a blacksmith and whitesmith in 1856 by Dawson White, son of Edward White who was a farmer at Bicker Marsh. He lived at 7, Mill Hill.

A skilled craftsman, he made a variety of ironwork pieces, including an ornate panel for Fydell House gate, and a Communion Rail for Boston Stump.

In 1891 he built a Penny Farthing cycle, and rode it to Sutton Docks.

His son, Edward White (known as "Ned") took over the business in 1892 and in 1897 began making bicycles called "Whites Imperial" which sold for 13 guineas each. These premises were then known as "Imperial Cycle Works". He went on to make mechanically hand operated bath chairs for invalids and the first motor cycle in Boston, "White's Imperial Motor Cycles", which had a top speed of 28 mph. It was modelled on a Singer, with its engine in the back wheel.

Edward White

In 1917 Harry White Crampton, grandson of Dawson White, became an apprentice with the company, then joined the RAF during the First World War, flying Bristol F2B fighter aircraft. He subsequently returned to the family business after the war had ended.

During the 1920's the business expanded into the new world of the motor car and additional premises were purchased at the rear (previously occupied by Rout Green Old Brewery Yard; Framlingham Egg Co.; Samuel Waddington and Sons, tanners and hide market; and Beaulah's Canning Factory) to create workshop space.

Edward White Ltd., became agents for Singer, Citroen, Essex, Chevrolet, Bean, Buick, Armstrong Sidley, and was eventually the General Motors and Vauxhall Bedford main dealer.

At the time, there was a single kerbside petrol pump dispensing 6 grades of petrol.

In 1932 Edward White opened a new branch showroom at 49 Westgate, Sleaford, and there was further expansion at Boston, to include 56 Wide Bargate.

1939 saw the death of Edward White, at the age of 76. Mr. White had lived at "Ashleigh", Horncastle Road, Boston. The business was continued by his nephew, Harry White Crampton.

1949 Jowett Javelin and Bradford Vans were added to the agency stable.

1954 Ray Hadwick, nephew of Harry Crampton, joined the family business.

1956 further expansion came in the form of the new Mayflower Service Station at London Road, Boston which was opened in the Centenary Year of the business.

1969 Another new venture started at Kirton Holme with the Pre-Test Station for commercial vehicles.

By this time the original blacksmiths had grown into a huge motor business in both Boston and Sleaford dealing in all manner of vehicles, both new and second hand with facilities for servicing and repairs.

Edward White Ltd

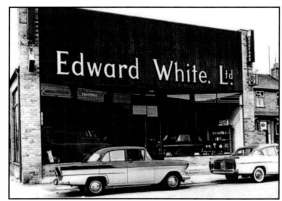
Vauxhall MDO 373

This car, a Vauxhall Cresta MDO 373, was owned by Harry Crampton, who sold it to Dudley Bryant's father, Freddie Bryant. Dudley was taught to drive by his Dad and passed his driving test in it at the first attempt.

1975 Harry Crampton retired, and Walter Woodthorpe Ltd of Boston, whose chairman was Alan Foster, gained a majority shareholding in Edward White Ltd. The business continued to trade as before with Ray Hadwick, as managing director.

1975 Walter Woodthorpe sold Edward White Ltd to Robert Wilson of Wilson Motors, Datsun Dealers, who continued in the motor trade.

1980 The site was sold to Tesco for redevelopment, Imperial Works being demolished, later becoming Gateway Supermarket, and ASDA Supermarket until it moved to Sleaford Road.

1977 Ray Hadwick left Edward Whites after 23 years to join Holland Brothers and become manager at their Skegness Branch.

1992 Ray Hadwick established his own firm at Old Leake, Hadwick Motors which continued until 2003 when he redeveloped the site with residential properties.

Ray Hadwick

In earlier times the Edward White frontage has seen Andrew Mitchell, pharmacist; William Lock, chemist, druggist, tobacco and cigars, and agent for Raynor's sheep ointment and McDougal's sheep dipping composition. He also sold pure vinegar and pure arsenic.

62-64 Wide Bargate

Elkington McKay

Chartered Accountants.
The partnership of John Elkington and Sarah Mckay followed Odling Elkington in April 2014.

John Odling, trading as F. Odling and Co, moved to 68 Wide Bargate in 1965 and John Elkington joined the partnership in 2008 when they moved to No. 62.

Elkington McKay

John's Father, Frank Odling was company secretary at William Sinclair and Sons Ltd., until 1948 when he resigned his position to start his own business, practising as Frank Odling Accountant in Boston Market Place. Son John joined him in 1957, becoming a full partner after qualifying as an accountant, taking over as Principal in 1990. John Elkington, after leaving Boston Grammar School, joined in 1966, and on Frank Odling's death was appointed manager, and then partner.

Previously, these shops have included G. Mableson; Kenneth. W. Sands, confectioner and general stores in the 1950's, later T. L. Sands & Son (also at 54 Argyle Street); followed by L. C. Hazell, confectioner and tobacconist; Carr's mortuary and chapel of rest, having been converted from two houses. Later it became Jane's Party Shop.

64 Wide Bargate

Previously, Carr's mortuary; Mrs Green's travel agency; Timothy Guy Ladies' Fashions (later moved to West Street and recently to Petticoat Lane).

66 Wide Bargate

Occupiers have included Bargate Restaurant; Harold Peatling Smaller, fish and chips and shopkeeper; E. C. Smaller, general stores; Sue Whaley, gangmasters.

68 Wide Bargate

Occupiers have included George Davey and Henry A. Burton.

Addaction

66-74 Wide Bargate
Addaction

Established 45 years ago, the UK's leading drug and alcohol charity, helps people with drug and alcohol problems. It also offers needle exchange; formal intervention team; criminal justice service; harm reduction and counselling.

'Prospect House'. Framework Young Persons' Accommodation Service, a charity which funds accommodation for young people is also in this building. This was formerly Teamwork Employment Agency.

Most Bostonians will remember these premises being owned by J. Carr & Son.

J. Carr

In 1893 this then belonged to D. White, cabinet maker, and was followed in 1909 by the establishment of the Carr family business by Joseph Carr. Joseph's father came from London travelling from place to place as an itinerant joiner ending up in Boston and started as a joiner and picture framer. This developed into cabinet makers, undertakers, funeral directors, and builders. This is one of the oldest local Boston businesses. Cabinet maker and Joiner by profession, including undertakers, picture framing, glazing, lawnmowers, DIY, tools and ironmongers. Joseph also made dolly tubs.

During the Second World War Carr's were coach builders, making the rear part of army lorries supplied by Edward Whites.

David Carr's father, Sidney, made car and lorry windscreens by hand, and was renowned for his freehand glass cutting. He also conducted 350 funerals each year with handmade coffins. He claimed that his undertaking skills made him the best 'boxer' in town.

Reg Thornton traffic policeman was promoted to detective sargeant and came to Boston in 1930, under Chief Constable Norman Frost. Reg's wife was manageress at Russell Allen's ladies' dress shop at the corner of High Street and Bridge Street.
In 1947 he established Creamline Taxis, which he subsequently sold and then in 1969 he purchased Carr's funeral undertaker's business with his son, Brian and Albert Bond. They retained the business name, and later moved across the road until 1992 when the business relocated to premises in Spilsby Road, just across Bargate Bridge which used to be Coppins, and the Queen's Head public house until it was demolished to make way for the widening of Bargate Bridge.

The growth of supermarkets, DIY stores, builders' merchants and mail order firms began to affect the tool and ironmongery business which led the Carr Family to continue the residual business of power tool suppliers; lawnmowers and garden machinery sales and service.
In 1999 David Carr officially retired, (but he still goes into work every day) and handed over the business to the fourth generation of the family, and current directors are Charles Anthony Carr (MD), David Matthew Carr (internet sales) and Catherine Louise Carr (finance director), the business now being operated from 10 Horncastle Road. The advancement of the internet presented a whole new opportunity, and brought the start of a successful new era.

Earlier occupiers of 72 and 74 Wide Bargate, when it was two properties, included George Henry James, plumber, glazier and heating engineer; F. W. Swain, paints and wallpaper; A. D. Johnson.

Here was the access to the rear of Edward Whites Garage, followed by 1 Horncastle Road, which was Edward White's second showroom, subsequently demolished to make way for the new Gateway Supermarket which became Asda, including 76-78 Wide Bargate.

Bargate End

This is the name given locally to the northern end of Wide Bargate, around the area of the current roundabout at the junction of John Adams Way, Bargate Bridge, Wide Bargate and Horncastle Road.

80-82 Wide Bargate is probably the rear of Enderby's and outbuildings of Waggon and Horses pub.

Carrs Funeral service and mortuary was converted from two houses when it moved here from No. 64 across the road, before moving again to its current base at Holman House, 2 Spilsby Road.

First floor and outbuildings of Waggon and Horses Public House

George S. Hiom
Carpets, Bargate upholstery works.

Peter Hiom, son and partner of George Hiom, recalls the fascinating family story.

In 1943 Sydney Robert Hiom, his wife Louisa, daughters Flo, Bett and Amy and son John moved from Leytonstone in the East End of London, to Spalding to escape the blitz as German aircraft bombed the capital. The family soon moved to Boston. Their other two sons, George and Sydney (Syd) were away serving in the British Army.

Father Sydney, got a job on the Boston Central Park-keeper's staff and was affectionately known as 'Old Man Hiom'. The men in the family were keen sportsmen. George, as a youngster, played cricket and football, but he excelled at football and played in the Football League. Syd was a very talented cricketer but sadly service cut short the prospect of playing county cricket for Essex. When the war in Europe ended in 1945, both George and Syd joined the family in Boston while Jack returned to his roots in London.

Both George and Syd served in the Army in Europe and George is reputed to be one of the first Allied troops to land on the Normandy beaches on D-Day.

On returning to their family, George, a skilled upholsterer, went into the upholstery business and opened a shop at 78 Wide Bargate, which was part of the Waggon and Horses public house. Syd worked as a machinist at May and Hassell, timber merchants in Skirbeck Road. Both played cricket in the Boston and District Cricket League in the 1950s to 1960s for Vauxhall Cricket Club.

However it was as a Boston Town Cricket club member that Syd became famous. It is fair to say that in the 1950s and early 1960s he was Boston Town Cricket Club's most outstanding batsman. He went on to play for Lincolnshire for many years in Minor Counties cricket. He was an elegant batsman, who is recorded as scoring 1,000 runs in one season, a brilliant cover point fielder and an occasional slow spin bowler.

Peter Hiom became a partner in the business, the company name changed to G. S. Hiom and Son and in 1970 moved to 14 South Street and in 1992 to Nelson Way, the company closing February 2015.

Peter is a keen golfer and plays regularly at Boston Golf Club where is son, Nick, is the club professional.

Peter's wife, Christine played indoor bowls for England from 1991 to 2001, becoming Ladies National Singles champion and also won the British title in 1991 in Belfast. She also had an eye for business, being the owner and operator of Rachel's Kitchen in Church Lane, Boston. She sold the business in 2014.

Another family member to make her name in Boston is the well-known and loved local jazz singer, Ann Smith. She is Syd Hiom's daughter, who was adopted by her aunt, Amy Smith. Members and supporters of Boston Jazz Club need no reminder of her talent and long service to the club and jazz music.

In 1893, D. White, Blacksmith operated from 78 Wide Bargate.

84 Wide Bargate

Enderby's of Boston

Opticians and Optometrists

Enderby's is a family run independent business, first established in Boston in 1907.

Founded by George Enderby, Enderby's was one of the only opticians in Boston and the surrounding area. From the very beginning, George wanted to provide the best eye care possible and he was one of the first opticians in the country to receive a formal qualification with a background in pharmacy and maintained an excellent level of professional care until his retirement.

84 Wide Bargate - Enderby's Opticians

Philip and Deborah Enderby

It is son John M. Enderby, consulting optician, that followed in his father's footsteps.

John developed a glazing facility within the practice, the first in Boston, which allowed the Enderby's technicians to hand finish lenses on site and to provide a same day service.

Philip Enderby was the next to join the family practice in 1967, working alongside his father John. He was one of the first graduates in Europe to obtain a degree in Optometry.

Philip introduced contact lens fitting to the town, and is one of the few opticians in the area to be awarded the DCLP (Diploma in Contact Lens Practice). His expertise has continued in this field and his knowledge and experience is constantly sought.

Philip has supervised many optometry graduates during their pre-registration years and has helped prepare them for their professional examinations. He continues in practice with his wife Deborah, the practice manager.

Deborah joined the practice in 1993 and has overseen the complete modernisation of the practice image. Her new look for the interior, and her introduction of the brands and designer frames that they promote alongside the clinical services on offer ensure that Enderby's continues confidently into the future.

Lisa Hardy, Philip and Deborah's daughter, joined the practice in 1994. She qualified as a dispensing optician in 1997, the first in the Enderby line to do so, and is the senior dispensing optician.

In 2008, Ben Enderby, Philip and Deborah's son, joined the practice. Working alongside Deborah as a practice manager he has moved Enderby's into the digital age. All systems have been computerised allowing seamless transfer of information throughout the practice. Ben has designed the company website, and is responsible for marketing and social media.

86/88 Wide Bargate - David Hallgate

Richardsons

86/88 Wide Bargate

David Hallgate

Optometrists and Contact Lens practitioners.

Established in 1994 by David Hallgate, with practice manager Mrs Julie Hallgate, following the previous 1980 partnership of Enderby & Hallgate Opticians, trading from this and the adjoining property.

The building dates back to the 1800's, having been a Grocers, J. and J. Beaulah's and a Butcher's shop and 'The Furnishing House' owned by Arnot Richardson in the 1950s and 1960s.

90 Wide Bargate

Passion Hair Design

Senior Stylist, Alica Hallowinski, took over from Syd Bolland four years ago.

From the 1930s this has been Leonard Borrill (or Burrell); E. Borrill, general dealer and milkman; Eric Lammie, hairdresser; Syd Bolland, who used to have a salon in Main Ridge before John Adams Way was built and the premises had be demolished.

Syd served in the Navy Special Service during the Second World War and was on the Normandy beaches before the landing of Allied troops.

Passion Hair Design

90 Wide Bargate

Time to Time

Fine Art gallery and framing service.
Established in 2005 by Miss Tammy Smith, earlier occupiers have included W. H. (Bill) Stanwell, Butcher, in the 1950s and 60s, previously Dowse's butchers; Bruce Alexander and Co (Boston) Ltd., insurance brokers (David Reynolds); Elegance Shoes; Oasis Hair Teams.

90 Wide Bargate - Time to Time
and 94-96 The Roadhouse Music Store

94-96 Wide Bargate

The Roadhouse Music Store

Musical instruments and sheet music retailers.

Owned by Mr. Andrew Bell from the late 19th century to about 1970 this was Andrew & Co., poultry foods, corn dealers and animal feeds, with Andersons Mill Shop. The last proprietor was Ralph Sylvester who also owned Anderson's Mill in Cheyney Street, now the car park behind 55-59 Wide Bargate.

98 Wide Bargate

The Flower Shop

Owned by Mr Wells of Sleaford.

Previously this was Heather Shaw, florist, followed by Fleurtations, the local florist, first established by Brian and Becky Thornton and created out of part of the Waggon & Horses public house.

The Flower Shop

100 Wide Bargate - Brian James Accountants

100 Wide Bargate

Brian James, FCA Chartered Accountant

A Boston Grammar School old boy, Brian served his articles with Hodgson Harris and Co, qualifying as a chartered accountant and joining Lucas and Sharpe, 5, South Square, Boston in 1979, becoming a partner in 1981. When they sold out to Dexter & Co. of Horncastle, he set up business on his own account at 45, Wide Bargate, supported by faithful clients. The business expanded and moved to 100, Wide Bargate in 2013. Another local family business with his wife Susan, and his son, Andy, also a chartered accountant. Brian James has been a stalwart supporter of Boston United from 1957 to 1990, having been appointed a director by Chairman Pat Malkinson, also serving under Sydney Burgess and Jon Sotnick.

Brian James, Accountant

Previously this property was occupied by Hamshaw and Co., chartered accountants whose principal was David Hamshaw. In 2013 David Hamshaw moved offices to join Dexter and Co. at the Old Vicarage, adjacent to the Stump and Blenkin Memorial Hall.

Many will remember these premises as the Waggon & Horses Inn.

When the pub closed in the 1970's, it was purchased by Syd Budge, the local builder, who refurbished it into offices, and the Fleurtations flower shop.

Landlords have included R. Foster, Johnny Cuthbert, the World Champion Lightweight Boxer, Harry Russell, and Tony G. Charlton.

Johnny Cuthbert was born in Sheffield in 1904, a professional boxer becoming British Lightweight and Featherweight Champion, as well as an outright winner of a Lonsdale Belt. He fought 159 contests winning 112, including 33 KO's. After retiring from boxing he came to Boston, and was landlord of the Waggon & Horses, as well as the Indian Queen in Dolphin Lane, the Mill Inn on Spilsby Road, and the King's Head at Kirton.

Johnny Cuthbert

Here is Bargate Bridge

Bargate Bridge spans the Maud Foster Drain which was built in 1568. In those days before mechanisation men dug out the clay with large shovels, passing it from hand to hand up ramps to the top of the bank. It was first known as Maud Fosters Gowt, and replaced the old Scire Beck to reduce flooding of the fens north of Boston.

Richard Foster was a coal merchant and ship-owner, and when he died in 1563 his widow Maud carried on the business until 1581.

She owned other land through which the Maud Foster Drain was cut - from Cowbridge to Skirbeck Church, a distance of three miles.

Bargate Bridge Plaque

Bargate Bridge was built in 1805 by John Rennie (who also built the Town Bridge). It was widened on the south side during 1972-73 for the Department of the Environment as part of the road improvements to build the Boston Inner Relief Road (John Adams Way), and reopened on 26th April 1973 by Councillor Norman H. Hughes, Mayor of Boston.

Bailey House was demolished together with other properties including Towell's Timber yard and head offices.

Also demolished was Universal Tyre Company Ltd., tyre distributors, C. A. May & Son, sheet metal workers.

Bargate Lodge still remains, the remainder now forming the public car par.

J. S. Towell Offices and Depot

J. S. Towell Ltd

Timber Importers and Merchants established in 1917 by John Seymour Towell [1856-1938] lived at Hussey House, Skirbeck Road, son of Alderman William Towell (1837 -1914), former Boston Borough Councillor [from 1924-1938] Mayor of Boston in 1934, , followed by John Leslie Towell (1895-1976), former Boston Borough Councillor from 1950-1955.

The business grew and had 200 employees, before moving to Skirbeck Road and Boston Docks when Bargate Bridge was widened to cater for dual carriageway and leading to John Adams Way (Boston Inner Relief Road in 1978).

Prior to J. S. Towell, these premises were occupied as a dentist's surgery on the ground floor, which became the Towell's boardroom, with the secretarial office on first floor. In the centre of the frontage was the access to the yard at the rear. On the right at ground floor was their general office, with the managing director's office above.

At the rear was the timber yard, with a steam engine driving reciprocating saws, which was a very slow, but very accurate process.

Along the drainside was a two storey building, and steps down to the water's edge where the passenger ferry used to arrive from Wildmore Fen for market on Wednesdays and Saturdays.

Beyond this was Beaulah's pea canning factory. It was in the late 1800's that brothers John and Josiah Beaulah opened their first canning plant in the former cigar factory built by J. F. Smyth and Co., Later J. W. Thorns, and known as "Maud Foster Cigar Mills" alongside the Maud Foster Drain. John Beaulah was Mayor of Boston three times and made Alderman.

The Canning factory was closed in the 1960's (then owned by Wilf Beaulah, who used to live at Standish House, 120, Spilsby Road, Boston. This substantial house is now the home of Philip Enderby, optician). J. and J. Beaulah's sold out to South African Canners and Packers, who then sold on to Lockwoods of Long Sutton.

Towell's employed 120 men, and many more during the importing season. They also had timber yards on Skirbeck Road, and on Boston Dock.

Peter John Warren Towell, was the last Chairman and Managing Director of J. S. Towell Ltd., and on his retirement the business was sold to May & Hassell Ltd.

Beaulah's Pea Canning Factory

Mr Peter Towell

Born in Boston, Peter was educated at Miss Blight's school at Holy Trinity, followed by Boston Grammar School, and Stamford School.

On leaving Stamford in 1940 he joined the family firm as office boy, before serving in the Royal Armoured Corps and the Kings African Rifles in Nyasaland and Burma, achieving the rank of Major.
He was demobbed in 1946 and returned to J. S. Towell, with a spell of training with May & Hassell at Bedminster. He was appointed MD on his father's death in 1976. He was elected as Boston Borough Councillor in 1970 and was a member of Boston Rotary Club, Boston Rowing Club, Boston Rugby Club, and The Frogs Club de Petanque.

Boston Docks was one of the most important timber importing facilities in the whole United Kingdom, with several local companies competing for the trade.

These included W. H. Lewin, who started out as timber and hop merchants, becoming W. H. Lewin & Son when Frank Harrison joined the firm. In 1880 he took over and it became Harrison and Lewin. In 1917, James Tait became manager of the yards in South End (where the Royal Mail Sorting office is now) employing about 200 men.

Then there was E. S. Trenery, becoming E. T. Trenery & Sons of Northampton who employed another 60 men in Boston.

May & Hassell, a Bristol firm founded in 1885, opened up in Boston in 1928, under the management of Jack Atley, and ten years later was handling more timber than any of its other branches, employing up to 120 men in the height of the season.

All these companies handled general timber, but in addition there was Calders on London Road, who became a main UK supplier of timber telegraph poles. After the Dock opened, Mr Calder imported railway sleepers and built a creosoting mill on the Dock and in 1930, Sir James Calder extended the business into handling and creosoting telegraph poles. Within four years they were producing 45,000 telegraph and power line poles, sent to all parts of the UK.

The business developed further into Calders and Grandidge, also manufacturing roof trusses, and still operates from the London Road site.

Bargate Lodge
73 Wide Bargate

An early 19th century building, now converted into flats.

73 Wide Bargate - 19th century building converted to flats

The old Three Crowns Inn - converted into house/flats.

71 Wide Bargate

The old Three Crowns Inn was converted into a house/flats around 1970.

This was originally the off-licence for Colley's Brewery, which stood on the bank of the Maud Foster Drain. The original Three Crowns at No. 69, was demolished in the 1860's and the replacement Three Crowns was built at No. 71.

Landlords of the former pub have included John Young (1829); F. Watson (1893); D. Panton (1896); Flora Donnison (1919); William Wallhead, (also perhaps the Ram Hotel as well), Robert Harrison, Ann Stocks, Frank Wilson, Harry Craven, Walter Henry Porcher, Fanny Sayner, Victor Coward, R. Stanwell, Mary Rayton, John Wilson.

Holland House
69 Wide Bargate

Moulder's Dentist and Dental Surgery

Holland House was built around 1860, as was the Three Crowns Inn. Some 10 years later the name Three Crowns was revived and applied to a new pub next door, which was the entrance to Stainton's timber yard. Later in the early 19th century Colley's Brewery (later Dyer's), known as the Skirbeck Brewery, which was demolished and replaced as Thorns Cigar factory.

69 Wide Bargate - Moulder's Dentist & Dental Surgery

Interestingly, the original Three Crowns was owned by several Boston businessmen, Francis Thirkhill, Thomas Fydell, Clarke, and Gee (two of the richest men in Boston at the time).

In the late 19th century, Matthew Crowden had a boy's boarding school at Holland House, and on retirement rented it to Frank Thomas, who lived in the house, and manufactured mineral water in the outbuildings.

Matthew Crowden's

The present dental practice has always been a family affair, established by Reginald John Moulder, succeeded in 1958 by Eric J M Moulder who served as a dentist in the Second World War, and now by Peter Moulder who succeeded his father in 1990. The heir apparent is Rebecca Beck, Peter's daughter, who currently lives and works as a dentist in Yorkshire, and who might well be the fourth generation at Holland House.

Former Thomas Mineral Water Factory

Thomas Mineral Water factory

Now converted into Flats, but everybody in Boston knows this property as Thomas' Mineral Water factory, the name is still emblazoned on the side wall for all to see.

John H. Thomas was a chemist in the Market Place making soda water, amongst the medicines and decided to expand in about 1900 into these Wide Bargate premises. He was a Justice of the Peace, landowner, wine merchant, soda water manufacturer and chemist.

The business was well known and respected. Major Bettison married one of the Thomas sisters, and eventually sold out to Bill Harrison. J. H. Thomas and Sons Ltd. was then bought by Jack Blades and Geoff Snade in 1968, who continued to run the business till 1994.

Geoff Snade played football for Boston United from 1954 to 1965, whilst still running the business full time. He played left full back, and was in the team which caused a sensation by beating Derby County 6-1 in a memorable FA Cup tie in 1955. In the next round United were drawn away to mighty Tottenham Hotspur and were beaten 4-0 at White Hart Lane. The crowds at these two matches were 27,000 and 46,000 respectively. Amazing! Geoff played against some famous football names, including Stanley Matthews, Danny Blanchflower, Len Duquemin, Bobby Smith, and Geoffrey Norman

When Bill and Geoff retired and sold out to Bellamys in 1994, the building, owned by Moulders was converted into residential apartments, but still happily maintains the "Thomas Mineral Water" inscription painted on the side wall.

67 Wide Bargate

Currently vacant and for sale, latterly occupied by Chef Canton, Chinese restaurant and takeaway.

Previously it has been Sherwin Reynolds, the Boston builders, later taken over by Simons of Lincoln; Key Estate Agents; Boston Hi-Fi Centre; MG Car Club Headquarters; Boston Tool Hire; Photocopy Shop.

67 Wide Bargate - currently vacant

65 Wide Bargate

Hutsons

Sign manufacturers.

The Hutson family business moved here from 11 Wide Bargate in 1995. The "Ironmonger" was dropped from the name, and the business developed into sign making, together with Hutson's cook shop. New workshops were built in 2005, and the cook shop closed in 2009, leaving the great grandsons of Henry Hutson, Doug and Alex, building up a successful sign manufacturing business, specializing in vehicle graphics and digital printing.

65 Wide Bargate - Hutsons

Hutsons have been selling signs since 1913 and still retain an old invoice for an engraved dog collar!

Today's business has many local and national customers, making signs to order for all purposes.

This building originates from 1850, and was built by Mr. William Stainton. Next door was a stonemason. These premises, and No. 67 Wide Bargate was Sherwin Reynolds and Son Ltd., building contractors, managed by Mr. Alf Satelle, going back to at least 1934 and Walter Reynolds before that. In the late 19th century, Samuel Sherwin was the leading architect and builder in Boston, and many fine houses and other buildings by him are still doing good service.

63 Wide Bargate

Vacant

NFU Mutual have recently moved to Quaker House. Insurance Agents, originally by founded by seven farmers in 1910 to offer insurance at cost price to farmers. In 1998 they began insuring individuals and businesses outside the farming industry, and now operate from 300 branches around the country with a premium income of £1,200 million, with some 900,000 customers.

63 Wide Bargate - Vacant

In Boston, NFU Mutual were in Mitre Lane, off Strait Bargate, from where they moved in about 2000.

These premises were previously occupied by Felix Computers [James Graves], and Frank Langstaff (Francis Langstaff Ltd.), signwriters, painters and decorators, who had been here from the 1930s. From the 1860s to the 1920s the premises was a veterinary surgery.

Here is John Adams Way

John Adams was President of the Unites States of America from 1797-1801, a prominent lawyer and public figure in Boston, Massachusetts.

The Boston Inner Relief Road, built in 1970s and costing £1.4 million, was named after John Adams. Following the opening of Haven Bridge in 1966, Strait Bargate was pedestrianised, until 2008 when buses were allowed to travel through the town centre again at walking speed.

Old Map of Bargate

Cheyney Street and Mill Hill

Mill Hill was a cluster of buildings situated at the top end of Wide Bargate roughly opposite the Red Cow Hotel and now a car park.

In 1640 it was described as "one piece of waste land in Bargate whereupon was lately one windmill and one tenement". 40 years later there were several tenements

Eventually, there were 14 houses, Harry Broughton's fish shop, Russell's' Banana Warehouse.

No. 1 Mill Hill was North Pole Public House, whose landlord in 1893 was Benjamin Inceley Sewell. This pub closed down in 1908. Also on Mill Hill were T. Hawling, boot and shoemaker; R. Eaves, stone mason; Smith's Cycle Shop.

There was a cycle park where you could leave your bike all market day for one penny (old money)!

North Pole Public House

Tony Ayre

Tony Ayre lived at Mill Hill, and his father was the first man to have taxis in Boston.

Mill Hill was demolished in 1959 to make way for the cattle market, Bull Ring, Pig and Sheep Pens.

Cheyney Street comprised perhaps some 40 residential properties, and Bayfleet Ltd., cycle, motor and electrical wholesalers, which were all demolished to make way for John Adams Way.

Bayfleet was relocated by the Ministry of Transport into what is now HSS Hire Company.

My Memories of Mill Hill

In the mid-1940's, I was an airman stationed at RAF Coningsby, and if there was one place on earth where one should go on a Wednesday and Saturday night (if one was not on duty) was the Gliderdrome in Boston.

There was also in Mill Hill, a Salvation Army Hostel, sponsored by Mrs. Sinclair, the same blessed lady who operated the Fighting Forces Canteen, where British and Allied servicemen and women could get a warm meal and a hot cup of tea for the princely sum of one shilling. The same applied at the Mill Hill hostel, which was run by the Gallant Major.

Mill Hill - Bargate, Boston

The Gliderdrome dances finished at 11pm, and all young airmen wanted to have the last dance with his, or someone else's, girlfriend. By some fiendish logic the RAF authorities and the Milson Bus Company of Coningsby agreed that the bus would leave from outside the Peacock & Royal Hotel in the Market Place at 11pm precisely. Hence the conflict between having the last dance, missing the bus, or doing the half marathon to Coningsby, or calling on the Major at Mill Hill.

Whenever there was some special band, say Joe Loss or Leslie Hutchinson playing at the Gliderdrome, the dancing and the entertainment could go on until midnight. That presented a problem to us. We had to be back on the base by 23.59 hours, otherwise we were presumed "AWOL", or "Absent Without Leave", which was a Court Martial offence. Most of the motor mechanics were Jamaican airmen, so a "Plan B" was devised, and implemented. If a vehicle came in for service or repairs on the day of the big night out at the Gliderdrome, the job would not be officially completed. This vehicle would be earmarked for transporting those Airmen in the know to Boston and the Gliderdrome. The mileometer would be tampered with, and at an arranged time the vehicle would be smuggled out on to the Dogdyke Road, where its passengers would be waiting. The next stop would be a spot on Mill Hill where Mowbray's lorries were generally parked.

On this occasion everything went according to plan until the party of Jamaican airmen returned to the vehicle parked at Mill Hill after midnight. What happened was two Mowbray's lorries had blocked in the RAF vehicle. There was plenty of pushing and moving but no way could we get the vehicle out. Then, to add to the problem, a policeman came on the scene and offered his assistance. The word got around that if he asked who the driver was and asked for his Form 658, the driver's authority to have the vehicle in his possession, all airmen would blend into the night and leave the Policeman alone with the vehicle – simply because to have a service vehicle without authority is a criminal offence. The person or persons would be charged with stealing and tried in a civil court. However, all is well that ends well. The Policeman helped to get the vehicle out. The airmen thanked the officer. They spent the rest of the night in their billets in Coningsby, and not in a jail in Boston.

Cattle and Sheep Market

Boston was a prosperous town, and famous for its wool trade. The original sheep pens were erected in the Middle Ages.

In the 19th Century, Wide Bargate, and the various lanes including Pen Yard, St. Peter's Lane, Threadneedle Street, and Crapley's Court, were well known for prostitution, especially around the times of the main cattle and sheep fairs.

The Stock Market was established in 1847, permanent livestock pens being erected in 1871. In May 1905, 30,000 sheep were sold by auction in one day. The Cattle auction ring was built in 1912 and remained in weekly use, every Wednesday, until 1974.

The former Cattle Market

There were also livestock auctions in the nearby towns of Spalding (Tuesday), Sleaford, Holbeach, Bourne (Thursday), Stamford (Friday), Spilsby (Monday), Alford, Louth (Friday) .Louth is the only one to survive today.

Auctioneers were Simons and Ingamells; Simons, Ingamells and Young; Mackinder, Bennett and Balderston; and Killingworth and Dunn.

Market business by the farmers and cattle dealers and butchers was done in the market or in the nearby pubs, namely the Woolpack, Red Cow, Cross Keys, Ram, Waggon & Horses, Three Crowns and the County Club

During the Second World War grassland was ploughed up to enable food production to be increased, and by the mid 1970s the big cattle trade was dying out.

During the TB outbreak in the late 1950s, a separate cattle pen was built to hold inspected animals.

The Cattle Market was closed down, buildings demolished, cattle pens removed, and the whole area converted into a public car park.

'A Bullock in the Bedroom' by J. G. Horton

Imagine the scene on a very hot summer afternoon around 1910 when all was quiet in Bargate End.

It was hot and sultry, and everyone who could, had put work to one side. Fred Staniland the barber was sitting in his shop doorway reading his newspaper. Tubby Wright the butcher and his man were sitting in the shop, with the window and door wide open, and the meat in the ice box. The Ram Public House doors were wide open; in those far off days the pubs could open from 6am to midnight. The vet Walter Dickinson had taken off his morning coat, and was fanning himself. His coachman Tom Harrison was standing talking to Tom Foreman at the Smithy, and there were others taking their ease. It was even too hot for us boys to play at anything energetic. In those days there were trees and grass around Mill Hill.

One lady who lived there was frequently "taken with the vapours" as she put it, and had to have another little tot of brandy. This trouble often occurred several times a day. Her house had iron railings around the little garden, and as she crossed over to the Ram for another little tonic, she left the house door and garden gate wide open. It was of no real concern, as from her seat in the Ram, she could see the house.

Suddenly the scene changed. A few bullocks were being driven from the Bargate Bridge direction, and the drover stayed to have a word with the Smithy.
The beasts, seeing a small patch of grass, went to it and after a moment the drover rather noisily tried to round up his small herd as they scattered. One of them bolted through the garden gate and house door and up the stairs. It came to a standstill wedged between the wardrobe and the bed. "Here was a pretty kettle of fish".

Everyone suddenly aroused from their rest and ran across to the scene, and a plan of action was generally approved. Tom Harrison fetched a long ladder from Dickinson's Yard. Bill Raithby fetched a big rope from the slaughter house in the Ram Yard. Tom Harrison broke the bedroom window and got in. Bill Raithby climbed the stairs and threw the loop of the rope to Tom Harrison who was standing on the bed, and he slipped the loop over the animal's horns; a light rope was also attached to one of the beats hind legs to encourage it to walk backwards. Meanwhile the frenzied animal was struggling to get free, and broke many things in the process. When all was ready, gentle pulling was exerted on the ropes and the animal very slowly responded and backed down the stairs. The filth and damage was indescribable. Meanwhile our lady had had to have a little more revival spirit, and was by this time in no fit state for anything. She was helped into Mrs. Goose's shop to sleep it off.
Meanwhile, willing hands with buckets of water and brushes cleaned up the worst of the mess and various ladies around and about helped clean up the house. So ended a hot summer afternoon.

61 Wide Bargate

This was on the corner of Cheyney Street and demolished to make way for the new roadway. It had been the well-known Tony's Snack Bar (Tony Farrow's Cafe) during the 1950s and 60s. Previously William Lines, grocer; Ernest D. Ayre, Shopkeeper; W. Shaw, bonesetter (attends on Wednesdays); G. W. Forinton, general stores.

59 Wide Bargate
Residential Flats

This was The Ram Public House in the 19th Century and before. The Landlord in 1893 was H. Budge; 1919, Edwin Littlewood; Herbert Overton; Ernest Edward Howes. It was owned by Soulby, Sons and Winch.

59 Wide Bargate - now residential flats

59 Wide Bargate - former Ram Hotel

The Ram catered for farmers and livestock dealers at Wednesday markets, together with other pubs including the Red Cow; Waggon & Horses; Queen's Head; Three Crowns; Cross Keys (now New England); North Pole.

In 1951 it was sold to J. W. Green of Luton, becoming The Aardvark, and when it declined in popularity as a pub, was purchased by Oldrids together with the then derelict Lincolnshire Fruit Importers warehouse at No. 51, and also the disused Andrews Feed Mill at the rear of No. 51.

After demolition of the last two and the incorporation of the rear of No. 59, Oldrids rebuilt a three storey three flat building incorporating a vehicular access to a car park at the rear. The flats were sold, and the pub was purchased by a developer and converted into flats.

57 Wide Bargate

Bella Hair

Three Boston ladies' Tracy, Charlotte and Catherine, went into partnership and opened as hair stylists in April 2014.

An earlier occupier was M A Labour, agricultural labour supply.

From 1904 until 1994, this was a family butchers, A. Wright and Son.

When David Wright speaks of 57 Wide Bargate he does so with some affection and humility. His great grandfather, Arthur, was a cattle dealer and butcher, and with his wife, Lucy Hannah Wright, opened a butchers' shop here in 1904.

When asked where Arthur Wright came from, he just said "Boston", for as far as he knew all the Wright family before him came from Boston. He is Boston born and bred, and proud to be so.

57 Wide Bargate - Bella Hair

A. Wright & Son

At first the Wright's of 57 Wide Bargate used the abattoir run by Lyell's at 33 Wide Bargate. They later progressed had their own abattoir in Field Street.

Albert followed Arthur, and then George, who served in the RAF during the Second World War, and then David succeeded, making him the fourth generation running this well-known family business.

With the shop and their own abattoir, the business expanded. George was a pig dealer of note, buying and selling in many markets in Lincolnshire, and supplying pigs to the Bilston Bacon Factory in Staffordshire.

David's first job with his father was slaughtering, boning, sausage making, washing up and scrubbing floors. Thanks to his father's tuition he became an experienced and professional butcher, but was not so keen on the "selling" aspect of the job in the shop. On father's retirement, David decided to change course. The advent of supermarkets prompted him to sell the shop premises, and concentrate on butchering and wholesaling from the Field Street abattoir, which was extended in the 1980s. They were supplying meat to shops in Skegness, Lincoln, Sleaford, Spalding, Norwich, London, Grimsby, and elsewhere.

But EU regulations meant that they were only allowed to kill 12 units of animals per week.

That is 1 beast, 6 sheep, and 3 pigs. Not enough to make a living, and EU regulation kept on raising the bar, so in 1994 David and his wife Pam made the most serious and complex decision the family had ever had to take, and move to new purpose built premises on the Riverside Industrial Estate at Nursery Road, where they would not be restricted to low turnover by EU rules. A huge financial loan was necessary, and many sleepless nights, but David joked that "It was that or getting a job at Tesco's"!

After 20 years his risk-taking has been successful. They now have four of the most up to date long distance vehicles delivering to customers all over Lincolnshire, and northwards to Grimsby, and southwards to London.

He talks in hundreds of tons when he speaks of meat deliveries, supplying under contact to Lincolnshire Co-Op, own label packet meat under Lincolnshire Quality Meat label, and servicing shops, pork for Boston Sausages, restaurants and hotels.

David says he can recall the days when there were 32 family butchers' shops in and around Boston.

Then, he saved the best bit till last, and invited Dudley and I to see their newest venture, "call it their 2015 risk", a custom built retail butcher's shop next door at Nursery Road only just opened to the public the day before. The Wright's are back in the retail butchering business, with top quality meat for us all to enjoy.

The future of the Wright family business seems secure for the future with David's two grown up sons, Andrew and Christopher, working with father in the business. Who knows, in another 111 years there could well be another family member conducting an interview about the Wright's, late of 57 Wide Bargate.

Following Wright's, this shop has been occupied by Pumpkin, a Children's Clothing and Maternity Wear Shop; Computer Shop; and an Employment Agency.

55 Wide Bargate

Rice & Spice

Takeaway restaurant.

Proprietor Ash Rahman opened in 2010, having moved from 15 Bridge Street, where he traded as 'Shapla' and has been in business in Boston since 1992. Born in Bangladesh, he came to England in 1982, attended Northampton Grammar School, and moved to Horncastle in 1989. His three children have studied English, Politics and Sport at their respective universities.

55 Wide Bargate has been a food establishment for most of the last 165 years. In 1850 it was a "cook shop", then a "dining room". In 1893 it was C. R. Gunby, coffee and refreshment house, then in 1930, Emma Hailstone's sweetshop, then A. Storr, cafe and general store, and Berry's Newsagents who also sold sweets.

55 Wide Bargate - Rice & Spice

Additional occupiers were Chattertons; Angelo Fiore, Italian Connection, takeaway restaurant; Ali Hairdresser, and Turkish takeaway.

53 Wide Bargate - Sim1nk

53 Wide Bargate

Sim1nk

Tattoo and body piercing studio.

Award winning male and female tattoo artists. Licensed, Health Registered.

Previous occupiers have been Frederick Staneland, hairdresser, William Meades, gents hairdresser; George H. Meades, gents hairdresser (affectionately known as "Slasher Meades"); Eve Whalley, ladies' hairdresser; Wilson's Gun Shop, guns and clothing, proprietors, Mr Ian Wilson and Mrs Angela Wilson.

51 Wide Bargate - now residential flats

51 Wide Bargate

Three privately owned Residential Flats

For many years, this property was Lincolnshire Fruit Importers, and the story of that local business starts and finishes with the Lealand family, which came from Old Leake.

George Lealand worked on the railways, but saved enough money to buy a cottage and an eight acre small holding in Old Leake. He also rented another six acres.

The cottage was without gas, electricity, and running water. The walls were made of mud (clay) and straw and the ceilings were so low that he couldn't stand upright.

Despite a very low income, the family still ate well, with good basic food. They kept chickens, a pig, and a cow. Their battery powered wireless was only switched on to hear the farming and main news.

His son, Arthur Lealand, was called up to serve in the First World War in Mesopotamia (Iraq) where he caught malaria. After the war, he and his father would take vegetables from the Old Leake smallholding on a horse and cart to sell in Wormgate at Boston. The 16 mile journey there and back would take four hours.

That gave Arthur the idea of opening a fruit and veg shop in Wormgate in about 1920.

Before marriage, his wife had been a well-respected personal maid and cook to Lady Winteringham at Little Grimsby Hall, a few miles north of Louth, and their first marital home was a two up and two down terraced house at the back of what is now Goodbarn's Yard pub in Wormgate. They built up the business and moved to 6 Red Lion Street which had the luxury of a bath and inside toilet, with a shop at the front.

Mrs. Lealand used her cooking experience to advantage by making jam, pickles, lemon curd and mincemeat, all being sold in the shop, and also selling to other shops in the villages.

Entrepreneurial spirit and ambition led to the purchase of land at Marsh Lane, where he built some glasshouses, whereby he could get a better income from a small area of land. All the produce was taken by horse and cart to the shop. He started growing flowers, and sold them for funerals.

Expansion continued by buying land at Halfway House, Fishtoft. He rented his land at Marsh Lane to a young man from Holland - that was Van Geest - who built up a multi-million pound business in Boston and Spalding.

A market stall in Boston on Wednesdays and Saturdays was added to the business, and the jam factory, fruit and veg retail and wholesale business supplied customers from Boston to Skegness, and all the villages in between. Goods were delivered by a 3 wheeler Van, later replaced by a 3 ton lorry.

Additional supplies were bought at Covent Garden market in London, and transported by a local haulier.

In the 1950's another venture was established by Arthur Lealand, together with Mr. Mowbray and Alderman Cyril Valentine. Lincolnshire Fruit Importers got involved with a Dutch exporter shipping goods into Boston Docks.

Former Lincolnshire Fruit Importers

The Second World War stopped nearly all imports of fruit and veg, but the farming business carried on.

Ray Lealand worked as a young man in 1937 for his father, Arthur, doing jobs like standing on the markets, etc.

In those days, the Boston Saturday market didn't finish until 10pm, but if there were any flowers unsold, Ray's father would tell him to stay on and try to sell them. But by that time at night the only buyers left were the drunks coming out of the pubs. But a few shillings was still better than dumping the flowers.

Arthur Lealand was a Borough councillor, and appointed an Alderman of the Borough in recognition of his outstanding service to the Borough.

On Ray Lealand's retirement, the Lincolnshire Fruit Importers business closed, the warehouse at 51 Wide Bargate was sold, the buildings demolished, and the site redeveloped with three modern apartments, retaining the vehicular archway now leading to the private car park at the rear. This was where the Cheyney Street Anderson's Mill, an animal food factory stood, in the old brewery.

It is thanks to Ray's 86 year old widow, Mavis, that this fascinating family story can be told.

In 1939 Ben Kent, Engineer was here, and in the 19th century it was the Eagle Brewery, being acquired by the Hundleby Brewery of Spilsby in 1920.

49 Wide Bargate

The New England Hotel

Owned by Regent Investments, this 3 star hotel offers traditional charm with 28 en-suite bedrooms, 120 seated restaurant, and the Pilgrim and Imperial Bars. There are ample facilities for wedding receptions, parties etc.

Proprietor is Mr. Imi Mian, with managers Mrs Margaret Kirk and Mr Valentine Shala.

49 Wide Bargate - New England Hotel

Formerly the Cross Keys Inn, owned by Holes Newark Ales. (The Cross Keys is a symbol of St. Peter, the Gatekeeper to Heaven).

In 1893 the landlord was J. O'Hara, and for generations this was a very well patronised market pub, eventually sold, refurbished and extended to become the New England Hotel by its new owners.

The Re-opening ceremony was a grand affair conducted by the Mayor of Boston, naturally on the busiest day of the week, Wednesday Market day with the cattle market in full flow. Brand new carpets and decorations were the pride of the new owners, but they had not appreciated the importance and needs of the cattle market habitués. They came in to have drinks and a look at the new pub, straight from the cattle pens and bull ring in their "dirty" wellington boots, leaving behind extremely "dirty" carpets!

Opposite the New England Hotel is the Cattle Market car park, owned by the Boston Borough Council.

This was the site of Mill Hill and the former Cattle Market with its Bull Ring and sheep and pig pens.

Corporation Yard, known as the Poultry Market

The Corporation Yard, known as the Poultry Market

In 1829 this was called Pen Yard where the wooden hurdles were stored between market days.

Today this is the car park for the New England, but from the 1930s to 1960s it was the Holland County Council Offices and Roads and Bridges Depot. Then Killingworth and Dunn's poultry auction moved here from Bargate Green in the 1970's.

Note the three crowns from the Boston Borough Coat of Arms on gateposts. The three crowns refer to the town's medieval links with Cologne, and the woolsack reflects the town's prosperity based on the wool trade.

St. Peter's Lane

Originally a terrace of Bede Houses, possibly occupied by M. Swaby; G. Dawson; A. H. Woodthorpe and others in the 1950's.

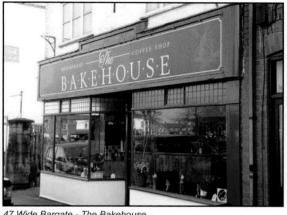

Poultry Market Gate Post

47 Wide Bargate
The Bakehouse

47 Wide Bargate - The Bakehouse

Opened in 2015 by Michael Wood, formerly Country Gourmet in Pen Street.

These premises have been operating as a bakery for 150 years under eight consecutive ownerships. In fact it is thought that there had been a bakery business at these premises since the 1850s.

Many will remember J. R. Panton (John Robert), baker and high class confectioner, and Mayflower Restaurant catering for luncheons, teas, dinners, wedding receptions and children's parties (1930); R. H. Faulkner (Bob) continued the tradition.

Robert Faulkner purchased this property and business in 1957 from Mr. J. R. Panton.

Born in Woodhall Spa, he started his career in baking at Chapman's, millers and bakers in New Leake and continued to ply his trade during his National Service in the Army.

On retirement, Robert sold the business to Mr. Livings of London, who in turn, sold on to Rob and Sally Billingham. It changed its name to Billingham's Bakery of Boston until 2014, and was followed by Starr's, flowers and coffee shop, opened on 12th May 2014, by proprietor Richard Starr.

45 Wide Bargate
Games Workshop

Fantasy and war games and gaming.

Opened in April 2010, the present manager, Mr. Johnathan Gaish, sells Fantasy table top miniatures; such as War Hammers 40,000; War Hammers Fantasy Battles; Hobbit and Lord of the Kings. It really is a fantasy store for youngsters and teenagers alike.

This was previously the home of Thorley the ropemaker, and then James Smith, plumber and ropemaker.

45 Wide Bargate - Games Workshop

In 1876 it was Edwin Nicholson, tea dealer and clock cleaner, and in 1891 becoming watchmaker and tobacconist. He died in 1893, at the age of 49 when his son Edwin James was only nine years old. The business was taken over by A C Kirby. Edwin James Nicholson, living in Carlton Road became a coal merchant's clerk and in 1906 moved to 45 Wide Bargate remaining there as Nicholson's Tobacconists until 1982. A C Kirby moved to 23 Wide Bargate.

More recent occupiers have included Britannia Insurance; Boston United Football Club supporters' Shop; Mortgages 2 Suit U.

First Floor Office - 45 Wide Bargate

Now vacant, but previously occupied by Brian James FCA, Chartered Accountant, who recently expanded into his current offices at Bargate Bridge.

Here is Pen Street

The Sheep Pens, Pen Street

45 Wide Bargate - European Food

43 Wide Bargate & 1 Pen Street

European Food

Groceries, wines and spirits, frozen foods.

Opened in October 2013 by Proprietor Dimitry Mustaman, and Manageress Julia Salkova.

Many years ago this was Hubberts Hairdressers, and then another Boston family business, Mablesons Ltd., grocers, wine and spirit and provision merchants traded from here from 1920s to the late 60s, when the owner, Jim Mableson retired and sold the premises to Coral Bookmakers.

After that, it became Collections Dress Shop.

41 Wide Bargate

Tiffany's Nails

The business was established 2011 by proprietor Tiffany Nsuyen.

However, from 1830 to 1900 there were two generations of Robinsons hairdressers here, then for many years, from 1939, this was the Army & Navy Stores, clothiers, and specialists in workmen's wear and owned by a succession of local businessmen including A. D. C Chesman, Cyril Maidens, and Phil Hazlewood. It then became The Great Dane Adoption Society, a Charity Shop, registered to Mrs Joy Ledingham.

45 Wide Bargate - Tiffany's Nails

The story of Cyril Maidens and The Army and Navy Stores is a special one.

Cyril was born in New York (Lincolnshire), his father worked for Lincoln's the seed merchants, who had a warehouse in South Square which is now The Sam Newsom Music Centre.

In 1949, and aged 15, Cyril was told by his father that he had got him a job at 41 Wide Bargate in Boston with Mr. Jack Chesman who, with his wife, ran a clothing store named the Army and Navy Stores. Cyril did not like the idea of working in a shop. He very much preferred working with his dad in Lincoln's seed nursery but he did what he was told, and turned up at 41 Wide Bargate. There was immediate empathy between him and the Chesmans.

41 Wide Bargate has a long history of being a clothing shop; selling Government surplus stock; before Jack Chesman, his father ran the business, and before that there was a Mr. Watson.

Customers were mainly farmers and farm workers, and the stock in trade was chiefly Wellington boots, great coats, trousers, shirts and underwear. Later on, casualwear appeared on the shelves.

The premises were owned by Mrs. Palmer of the Palmer and Bell family who ran a motor business and were main dealers on the main road at Butterwick, now Thurlby Motors.

Later on, the Chesman's purchased the freehold. Their neighbours were Mableson's the grocers at No. 39, and Trent Steel factors at No. 43 who sold motor parts, followed by Allen's Radio Shop, then Budge and Mableson.

Cyril stayed with the store, and was made a partner in the 1960's, taking over in 1974. In 1980 he bought the business and the freehold property, continuing to run the business on the same lines as the Chesmans until he retired and sold out to Philip and Barbara Hazlewood in 1997. His part-time assistant of 35 years, Marie Hicks, also retired at the same time.

Army & Navy Stores

A D C Chesman

Thursday 6th March 1997 13

rril Maidens — retiring from his Army and Navy ore after 48 years.

Cyril Maidens

Philip added printing of "Logo's on Shirts" to the business.

Cyril says in his 48 years at No. 41 Wide Bargate two particular things remained constant - there was never a telephone in the shop; and there was always an open coal fire heating the shop, which proved very popular with customers in the wintertime. He often wondered how the shop's annual fire insurance policy was always renewed without question.

39 Wide Bargate

Unisex Hairdressers

Partners: Mrs Nicola Harris and Miss Michelle Whetley currently run the business.

In about 1860, this was the Great Northern Public House, with a skittle alley at the rear. Then in 1893 it was Caleb C. Smith, photographer; followed by W. H. Frost and Ernest Gray.

By 1934 it had become Halley Stewart Chester, confectioner, then William Joseph Wray, photographer, followed by Adkins Building Contractors; Holland Electrical Installations; Mrs Palmer's sweet shop; Heads and Faces hairdressing and beauty salon.

39 Wide Bargate - Unisex Hairdressers

37 Wide Bargate

Tooth Booth

NHS Dental Surgery.

Prior to the Second World War, occupiers had included Everard and Son and Waterfields.

At the end of hospitilities in 1947 RAF pilot, Flight Lieutenant Edward Mableson returned to Civvy Street and back to the family home at 43 Wide Bargate. It was where he was born and brought up as a member of a long standing business family. His brother, Jim was in charge of the well-established family grocery business known as Mablesons.

Edward, known as Ted, decided not to join the family business, but to start a business on his own account.

37 Wide Bargate - Tooth Booth

He joined forces with colleague George Budge and established the company Budge and Mableson, electro mechanical engineers and retailers in premises at 24 Wide Bargate. George Budge was a trained electrician, so he concentrated on the outside development of the business, while Ted concentrated on the shop side.

In 1959, the business moved to 37 Wide Bargate, a property owned by the Mablesons but occupied by Waterfields. In fact the Mablesons owned the premises covering the postal addresses 37-43 Wide Bargate.

The company continued to grow and in 1999 it proudly advertised products and services to the community as follows: "Budge and Mableson" electro mechanical engineers and retailers established 1947 we offer the following – Wide range of lighting and bulbs; fires and fire surrounds; electrical appliances; fancy goods; lighting designs; authorised Miele sales and services; Nationally registered electrical contractors. Service and advice on all electrical matters.

My first dealings with Ted Mableson were in the late 1970's when I was a member of Boston Chamber of Commerce's Organising Committee, to put on the Boston Trades Fair in Central Park. He was then a Director of the Chamber and a Justice of the Peace.

Among the leading lights were David Wright (Holland Bros); Bob Isaac (Oldrids); Richard Lenton (Nationwide Building Society); Richard Johnson (Johnson's Seeds); Mike Jessop (Jessops china shop). In later years I met Ted on many occasions at Chamber board meetings and in my capacity as the Chamber's Membership Officer.

Budge and Mableson, a family electrical store steeped in history, and in my interview with his son and successor, Andrew, I was confronted with a fourth generation Mableson who was proud of the fact that the Mablesons are a well respected Boston family of many, many years standing.

Their links to Boston span the ages, and a visit to the Holy Trinity Church in Spilsby Road to see the family gravestones bears testimony to that.

The growth of the big supermarkets took away the shop's trade, and it closed in 2009.

There is still an electrical contractor's business operating from the rear of the premises in Pen Street, but Andrew is reconciled to the fact that he may well be the last of the Mablesons operating from the premises, as his children are following other professions. This unfortunately is the story of the family run businesses.

Photograph of Dick Giles, George Budge and Ted Mableson

Waterfields Ltd., Occupied this shop prior to Budge & Mableson

35 Wide Bargate - Bismillah Foods

35 Wide Bargate

Bismillah Foods

This international supermarket and grocery shop opened in January 2013, and sells meat, frozen foods, spices, etc.

Earlier occupiers of these premises were Nicholas Allen, maker of traditional wooden chairs from 1805 to 1842; then Blaydons and Agnes Mary Morris; Avril's Perfumery, Avril Foster; George H. Foster, ladies' hairdresser; Pilgrim Décor owned by Stan and Kay Brockbanks; Our Price Pet Stores; Medina Food Store , Eastern Deli.

33 Wide Bargate

F M Lyell & Son

Butchers' Shop

A Butchers' shop since 1842, the current business established in 1869 by William Lyell is 145-years-old, the oldest surviving family business in Wide Bargate.

William Lyell was followed by James Smith Lyell; Charles William (Billy) Lyell; Christine Margaret Dawson; Steven John and Paul James Dawson, now the fifth generation still running the business, with the sixth generation coming up in due course.

33 Wide Bargate - F M Lyell & Son

Steven, Jamie and Christine Dawson, F M Lyell & Son

Charles William Lyell was an air gunner flying in a Lancaster bomber during the war. He flew on 29 successful operations.

Billy bought and sold cattle in Boston Cattle Market until 1974.

Christine worked as a nurse and trained at Morlands, and worked later at Boston Post Office and telephone exchange for eight years. (Postmasters were Mr. Jack Upsall and Mr. Rainbow). She then took over the butchers' business as a partner with her mother after the death of father (Billy) in 1981.

They operated their own slaughterhouse and abattoir at rear of shop until 1992 when new EU regulations closed it down. Then bought meat from Wrights until the present day.

Today, the partnership comprises Mrs Christine Dawson, Steven Dawson and Jamie Dawson.

Corpus Christi Lane

Formerly being Water Lane and where there was a pub called The Bull & Magpie

31 Wide Bargate

Today - an empty shop for sale or to let

This had been a tailors', drapers' and ladies' outfitters before being owned by Mr Rysdale. These premises became the family business of Holmes Shoes.

31 Wide Bargate

In 1932, Mr. Jim Harwood set up his son-in-law Horace Holmes in a retail shoe business based on the sale of agricultural requirements, boots, wellingtons, and eventually shoes. Horace Hereford Holmes married Gladys Harwood in 1932.

During the Second World War Mr. Holmes carried out repairs for the military, so was exempt from National Service but carried out duties as a warden in the Air Raid Precaution Service (ARP).

Their children joined the business. June in 1950, and Ronald (Ron) in 1952, after completing his National Service.

Mr. Holmes bought the premises in 1948 for £1,500.

But in 1803 the plot of land on which No. 31 now stands cost just 10 shillings and sixpence (52.5 pence in today's money).

Ron and Horace Holmes

Mr. Horace Holmes died in 1990, aged 82, and was still at work only three months before his death. In the 1950's Ronald and June became partners and took over the business. Over the years there were a lot of alterations to the premises and the business progressed accordingly. After 69 years, the business closed in 2001, and Ron and June retired.

June is noted for her voluntary work, such as the Royal Observer Corps which she joined in 1968; 15 years service as a Special Constable. A big supporter of the Boston Stump. June is Boston born and bred.

Mrs. Gladys Holmes died in 2001, and Ron in 2009 after a lifetime in the business. In the early days they had a market stall selling shoe laces, pegs, studs and pieces of leather for customers to mend their shoes.

The shop was then rented to the Boston Bargain Centre trading as Pound Plus Shop, selling general household goods and Discount Store.

Lindum House

27-29 Wide Bargate

Bambridges Solicitors

Partners are Sarah Spencer, Paul Faunt and Graham England.

The origins of this legal practice began in 1953, when Edmund Roythorne, solicitor of Spalding, expanded into Boston at premises in Pump Square, between what is now Sharman Burgess, estate agents and Bairstow Eves, estate agents.

27-29 Wide Bargate - Bambridges Solicitors

In 1970, the premises of Anderson's Creamery at No. 29 were purchased for further expansion of the practice with George G. A. Whitehead as Senior Partner in Boston. George Whitehead was appointed a Judge in about 1975, having been joined by J. E Barry Hodgkinson, and followed by Phil Brewster and Leon Fidler. In 1980, Dennis Bambridge moved from Spalding to join the Boston office.

In 2000, Dennis Bambridge purchased the Roythorne business, being ably supported by existing personnel of Ted Coote and David Nicholson, and others until his recent retirement, with his partners now continuing the Bambridge name.

Some interesting local family names appear in the historical ownership of these premises. In the 1700s and 1800s there was John Ball, bricklayer, Richard Butler, Thomas Treditt, Thomas Dixon, Edward Hummings, Rev. John Banks, Rev. Wilson Banks, Thomas Tunnard of Frampton, Thomas Gee, Caleb Preston.

From 1842-1860 it was the home of auctioneer Edward Tewson.

The frontage building was constructed by Rev. John Banks, Grammar School headmaster as a boarding school. In 1825 it became Miss Green's School and then Miss Hill's Day's Day School.

In 1852, the Bull and Magpie Public House, which appears to have been at the rear of the present offices, was sold by David Jackson and John Castor and Thomas Wise to Thomas Wells Thorpe, spirit merchant, and James Grant, brewer.

This pub closed down in about 1874, became a warehouse, purchased by Edward Smith Smith, who immediately sold on to Emma Wood, becoming Woods Supply Stores. Adjoining land was owned by Samuel Tunnard.

Further occupiers of these premises from the 1870s to 1960s have been the Dentists, Edward Smith Smith from 1876; Smith & McTaggart (Edward Percy Smith LDS Eng., dental surgeon and Daniel McTaggart, LDS, RFPS, (Glas). dental surgeon, who owned a Rolls Royce motor car); and R W Skene.

In the 1950's to 1960's No. 29 was occupied by A. Anderson and Son, confectioners, known as Anderson's Creamery, and on his retirement it was added to the solicitors offices; for a time the front shop was an agency office for the Gateway Building Society and later the Woolwich Building Society Agency, before being incorporated into Bambridges.

Here is Threadneedle Street

25 Wide Bargate

Vacant

From 1855 to 1912 this was a butchers' shop, until becoming offices in the 1920s to 1960s. Records show occupiers being William H. Lunn, Offices, Clerk to Fishtoft Sub-Committee of Holland Local Pension Committee & Holland (Lincs) Assessment Committee; the Registered Office of Boston and District Chamber of Commerce; Munkman Child & Co., chartered accountants, and R. A. Lunn, insurance agent; Subsequently it has been Pilgrim Sports Goods, Fishing Tackle Shop until 2009.

25 Wide Bargate - Vacant

23 Wide Bargate

Manflower

Chinese restaurant and family business of Peter Lee.

Established about 30 years ago, this was one of the first Chinese restaurants' in Boston.

Previously this was A. C. Kirby & Co., Tobacconists, established in 1884, selling Steeple Jack brands of tobacco and cigars, cigarettes, walking sticks, and fishing tackle, and warm salted peanuts. Mr. Kirby was President of Boston Angling Association.

23 Wide Bargate - Manflower Chinese Restaurant

21 Wide Bargate - Shephard's Bakers Ltd.

21 Wide Bargate

Shephard's Bakers Ltd.

Bakers and confectioners and cafe restaurant

This family Business was established in 1882, in Skirbeck Road by William Shephard, and moved to Bargate about 110 years ago.

The property comprised a shop, house and bakery. There was an outside wooden staircase to the first floor above the bakery, to which flour was hoisted up in one cwt. bags. There was a shoot back down to ground floor into the bakery. The dough machine and flour sifter were powered by gas. The bread, pastry and cakes were delivered by cart to all parts of Boston.

George Howitt, a market gardener before he married Miss Grace Amelia Shephard, learned the bakery trade from scratch. He fought in the First World War and sadly was one of the heroes who never returned home.

In 1949 the premises traded as the well known "The Copper Kettle".

The Copper Kettle was the first to stock Coca Cola in Boston, supplied by G. N. Beaulah's.

In 2004, Peter Howitt, grandson of the founder, married Gwendoline Huskisson, and inherited the business from his mother Mrs Dorothy (Dolly) Edna Howitt, whose husband Joseph died in 1970, and who controlled the business for 34 years.

The Howitt family still control the business in the person of Peter Howitt's son, Joseph Howitt, and his nephew Stephen Scuffham.

From 1841 to 1896 this property had been a druggist and chemists' shop, owned in turn by George Sewell and William Lamplugh.

From 1725 Nos. 19 and 21 included an acre of pastureland to the rear, owned by Stuart Watts, a clockmaker. On his death the property was sold for £140. George Mastin, also a clockmaker, followed him, and may have built the houses in Mastin's Court with access through the archway, which is still there today.

Here is Mastin's Court

(Some Directories call this 'Hastings Court')

19 Wide Bargate

Great Dane Adoption Society

Charity shop.

This was established 2010 and relocated from 41 Wide Bargate.

From the 1930's this was Morley H. Moslin, ironmonger and farm suppliers, followed in the 1950s and 60s by the Bargate Pram Co., children's outfitters and then The Health Shop which provided health and beauty products.

*19 Wide Bargate
Great Dane Adoption Society*

19a Wide Bargate

The Sleep Shop

Beds and bedroom furniture.

Opened in 1998, this family business is owned by Mr Mark Graves, selling bedroom and home furniture. He also has a shop in Sleaford, 'Sleep to Go'.

The previous occupier was Cowan's Fabrics who moved here from 25 Strait Bargate.

19a Wide Bargate - The Sleep Shop

First Floor

Diane Carter hair and beauty salon

Established some 65 years ago, by Diane Carter the salon offers a complete range of beauty treatments and for the last 15 years has been owned and operated by Mrs Christine Marshall and Miss Helen Marshall.

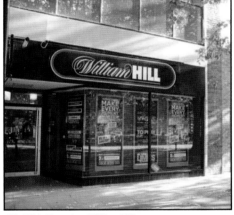

19b Wide Bargate

William Hill

National bookmakers.

National off-track betting shop. The company was established 75 years ago and has 2,300 betting shops across the UK.

19b Wide Bargate - William Hill

17a Wide Bargate

Coral Racing

National Bookmakers.

Previous occupiers have included William Hill bookmakers. Previously part of Waterfields, and earlier occupants included George Pycock, wheelwright; Chesman's Pram Co.; S. J. Borrill, fish restaurant; Bargate fish Cafe; Bargate Pram Company, prams, baby linen and children's outfitters.

In the early 20th century there was a substantial house on this site which was owned by Arthur Tuxford, physician and surgeon.

17a Wide Bargate - Coral Racing

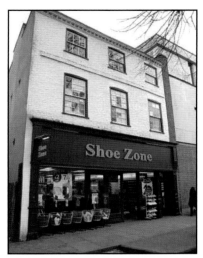

17 Wide Bargate

Shoe Zone

National shoe retailer.

In the early days the shop was called The Leicester Shoe King and its owner was a Mr. Wilford.

Cyril Jackson, now a widower aged 93, was manager of the Kettering and Leicester Boot Company shop in Boston.

He has quite vivid memories of his times at 17 Wide Bargate, where he started as an apprentice in 1935. After a six year break when he served in the RAF, Cyril returned in 1946 to continue his career in the shoe business.

17 Wide Bargate - Shoe Zone

When he returned in 1946 the shop was called Kettering & Leicester Boot Company. His business neighbours were Lingard's Music Store at No. 15, with the Tudor Restaurant, owned by Austin Skinner above it, and at No. 19 was the Grimsby Fish Supply Company owned by Mr. Borrill.

Cyril was soon appointed Manager, and swiftly promoted to area manager responsible for shops at Lincoln, Newark and Spilsby. He did not own a car, so he did his rounds on the train and bus, staying at hotels overnight. He never wanted to move from Boston. He well remembers the tank and cannons on display in Bargate.

Cyril was a prominent playing member of the Men's Own Social Club, and represented Boston at table tennis, snooker and billiards. He played alongside Cyril Howard, Ron Croft and Stan Johnson.

He recalls that when he started as an apprentice the shop opening hours were: Monday, Tuesday, Wednesday from 8.30am till 7pm. Thursday was half-day opening only in the morning. Friday 8.30am till 8pm. Saturday 8.30am till 9pm.

Other shoe shops in town including H. H. Holmes; Sterlings; Masons; Olivers; Freeman Hardy & Willis; Blindells; Dunns; Wyles; Benefit Shoe Shop; Bozeats; Co-Op; Meades; Belmonte.

From 1840 to 1905, this was a private house occupied by Reverend Richard Conington, and then by his widow. From 1891 it was owned by Mrs Mary Jane Philpott, probably his daughter. She was head of the household, but was called a lunatic, and had four servants – a housekeeper, a nurse, a housemaid, and a cook.

15 Wide Bargate

Now part of the Pescod Square Shopping Centre (Next Clothing Shop)

From the 1940's till 1960 this was the well-known Music Shop, simply referred to as "Lingards". Its full title being E. A. Lingard, musical instruments, music and television dealers.

Ernest Arthur Lingard and his wife Constance Mary came to Boston from Ramsgate in Kent. Ernest was a musical instrument repairer by profession. They were ardent musicians, Ernest playing the violin, and Constance the pianoforte.

Their first shop was at 77, West Street tuning various musical instruments, but primarily the piano. During the Second World War, the shop was totally destroyed when the Germans bombed West Street. This same air raid that demolished Lovely's Bakery, where the Massala Zone Indian Restaurant now stands.

Lingards Music - 15 Wide Bargate

The Lingards opened for business again further up West Street, and remained there till the late 1940's, when they moved to 15 Wide Bargate.

The property was rebuilt about 1950 by Allan and Newton and at the time, the shop window was the largest undivided window frontage in Boston. Lingards' also had another shop in Gainsborough.

The Lingards had two sons, John and David, who both attended the North London Polytechnic, qualifying as television service engineers, which enabled the family business to grow into the modern media age.

The shop sold all manner of musical instruments, sheet music, TV sets, records, cassettes, etc. The 1960's saw the advent of the Beatles, Rolling Stones, etc. and this rock 'n roll era led to the demise of the piano, and the growth of the guitar and electric organ. This period was the high point of Lingards' business and although there were other music shops in Boston, such as Hurst, Son and Page, and Allen's Radio, it is reasonable to say that Lingards was the town's leading music shop.

The shop was visited by many celebrities who were appearing at the Gliderdrome - in those days the mecca of pop music - including Ronnie Carroll.

Upstairs was the Tudor Restaurant and Cafe, run by Austin Skinner. Later in the 1960s it became the first Chinese Restaurant in Boston - The Oriental Restaurant, run by Aloysius Wong.

In 1960, the businesses closed down and the property was sold, to be redeveloped into Gateway Supermarket, later becoming Key Markets Supermarket, followed by the Pescod Square redevelopment.

In the early 19th century, this was a political powerhouse in Boston. Francis Thirkill being Town Clerk, his son was Mayor in 1826 and 1832, and his business partner as solicitors Henry Rogers, succeeded him as Town Clerk.

Thirkill and Rogers were both related to the Fydell Family, and were succeeded by Francis Thirkill White and John George Calthrop. White lived in the mansion at No. 13, with a huge garden which he bought in 1868 for £4,200. The White family still owned it until 1917, but by 1912 it had become an annex to Conway High School.

13 Wide Bargate

Next

Multiple fashion chain store.

Almost a century ago agricultural engineers, Grattons had a big impact on the town.

David Thomas Gratton was born in Hykeham in 1863, became an apprentice blacksmith aged 12. Later he started his own business in Nottingham then moved back to Lincoln, and in 1898 bought David Woods Blacksmiths at Lade Bank, Old Leake for £320. He sold it in 1920 for £600, having purchased 13 Wide Bargate in 1917 from Major White in an auction at the Peacock & Royal Hotel, conducted by James Eley.

13-15 Wide Bargate - Next

Gratton's

Mr. Gratton's sons and grandsons joined the business, known as D. T. Gratton & Sons.

In 1923 a new showroom was added fronting Wide Bargate. In 1921, Mr. Gratton provided a tractor which powered the Lincolnshire Standard's printing press and ensured that the paper was printed during the National Coal strike.

Among many others, he invented and patented a new hand pulled and wheeled machine for dry spraying insecticides, and later a horse drawn version.

In 1970 the Borough Council wanted to widen the adjoining Silver Street by demolishing Gratton's premises, so Alan and Peter Gratton relocated the business to a new site and buildings at Wyberton Chain Bridge. The Bargate premises were demolished and redeveloped as Gateway, then Keymarkets Supermarket and car park accessed from a widened Silver Street. This now also included No. 15 Wide Bargate. Keymarkets subsequently moved to larger premises at Bargate End, then taken over by Asda who moved again to Sleaford Road, where they are today. For a time it was occupied by What Everyone Wants.

The business flourished under the direction of Alan and Peter Gratton, grandsons of the founder, until they retired selling the business to Elgar. In turn they sold on to J. T. Friskney of Horncastle until they moved to their present site at Boardsides, selling the Wyberton Chain Bridge site for redevelopment into the present day Alban Shopping Park, opposite Oldrids Downtown, with Homebase, recently closed to become B & M, and Maplin. Previous occupiers have included a Carpet shop; Currys; Dreams and Comet.

The Bargate supermarket development was originally planned by Peter Firmston- Williams, son in law of Wilfred Beaulah. He was sacked for building too big a store!

Prudential Assurance offices were on the first floor.

Here was Silver Street, previously known as Thieves Lane, leading to Main Ridge and Pump Square, now the Pescod Square entrance.

One of the memorable properties in Silver Street was the Mason's Arms.

The site was a mason's yard owned by John and Thomas Rawson. He sold to George Hartley, who built a tobacco and snuff factory, and a house, for himself, and after his death it became the Mason's Arms Public House in about 1870.

During the 1859 Smuggling Riot, it is generally believed that contraband goods were received here by Mr. Smythe who had a grocery shop in the Market Place, and the cigar and tobacco factory at Bargate End.

In 1893 the Mason's Arms landlord was Alfred Mitchell, then George Frederick Dawson who went into receivership in 1900. He was followed by Walter Lee.

When I came to Boston in 1949 the Mason's Arms was owned and operated by Thomas Kitwood & Sons Ltd., wholesale grocers and wine merchants. The principal was Mr. Peter Kitwood.

It was known for its high quality and reasonably priced beer, and its service. It was patronised by many of the town's "well-to-do citizens", and the "watering hole" for Lincolnshire Standard staff members, amongst many others.

The last Landlords were Irene and Edwin Parker, and in 1966 the freehold and buildings were purchased by Oldrids who wanted the space for expansion and a car park, with an eye on future shopping centre redevelopment.

The pub eventually closed in 1971, and the news that the Mason's Arms was due for demolition to accommodate a car park was not well received by some of the patrons who showed their displeasure by painting impolite graffiti on the building.

Today the site is included in Pescod Shopping Centre.

Pescod Square Shopping Centre

In 2003 Silver Street and adjoining properties from various ownerships were acquired by Centros Miller and developed into a modern new shopping centre of some 93,177 square feet of retail space, with 20 shops and 400 space car park accessed from Pen Street, at a cost of £21 million.

Pescod Square Shopping Centre

Pescod Square won a Civic Design Award from Boston Borough Council in November 2004, a British Council of Shopping Centre's Gold Award in 2005, and a Civic Trust Award in 2007.

The new shopping precinct was opened in the summer of 2004 with original tenants including Next, Costa Coffee, Clinton Cards, Officers Club, The Works, All Sports, Superdrug, QS Family Wear, Peacocks, Wilkinsons, Home Bargains, Insiders, Bakers Oven, Stead and Simpson, HMV, Thomas Cook, Julian Graves, O2, Gamestation, and Ottakar's.

Since 2004 various tenants have occupied shops in this precinct, and then closed down, to be re-let again.

Some of the Shops in Pescod Square Shopping Centre

In 2015 the occupiers are Next; Costa Coffee; Vacant (formerly Clintons); Officers Club; The Works; Select; Superdrug; Bon Marche; Wilkinsons; Peacocks; Poundland; Pescod Hall (vacant); Greggs; EE / T-Mobile; Vacant (formerly HMV); Thomas Cook; James Edwards; O2; Game.

Pescod Hall is part of a house built in the mid-15th Century, formerly the home of the wealthy Pescod merchant family. The doors opened into the Great Hall. It was subsequently purchased by Oldrids in 1940. It was Adrian Isaac who, with members of his family, personally took the building apart in 1974-5, cleaned all the bricks by hand, and then rebuilt it, again with his own hands. It was later "picked up" rotated through 180 degrees and moved 20 metres on the back of a special computer controlled trailer to accommodate the new layout of the Pescod Shopping Centre, to where it now stands. New timbers were required and prepared by Oldrid's joiners, whilst Adrian repaired all the old ones for re-use.

This new shopping mall linked Wide Bargate and Mitre Lane via Silver Street with Petticoat Lane and the Market Place, and incorporated Pescod Hall, still owned by Oldrids, who had their young fashions department in the building until the construction of Pescod Square, Insiders Clothes Shop, followed by Espirit Designer Clothing and then let Subway Sandwich Bar.

Centros Miller is an urban regeneration property specialist with particular focus on retail and mixed use developments. Other projects by them have been in Kidderminster, Bury St. Edmunds, Blackpool, Islington, Maidstone, Chesterfield, Greenwich, Hoddesdon, Preston and Watford.

They are now owned by Sovereign Land and working in Portsmouth, Durham and Southampton.

Cattle Drive through Strait Bargate

11 Wide Bargate

Waterstones Bookshop

National chain of booksellers.

Formerly Ottakars - another renowned bookshop - who was the first tenant here when Pescod Square Shopping Mall opened.

Hutsons advert

11 Wide Bargate - Waterstones Bookshop

However, No. 11, Wide Bargate is likely to be referred to by local people as "Hutsons" for decades to come.

This property was built in about 1780, and was a public house called The Woolpack Inn. Some of the original stairs still exist on the second floor.

The pub closed after 1856, and from 1861 to 1882 it was occupied by Richard Linton, draper, silk mercer, milliner and dressmaker.

In 1885 it was R. Walker, draper, and then Robert Munkman, a tailor, lived there with his family, having relocated from New Street. R. A. Munkman and Son became general dealers and marine stores.

In 1900, Holland Bros. at 24 Strait Bargate, next to the Red Lion Hotel, decided to sell their ironmongery business, and the Hutson brothers, Henry and William, from Bury St. Edmunds, purchased it in 1905. Sadly William had died when they moved to these "more commodious" premises at the corner of Wide Bargate and Silver Street, which he bought from Robert A. Munkman & Son.

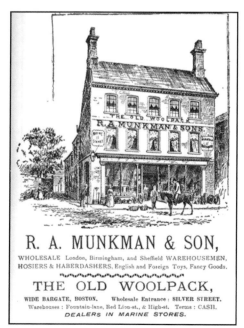

R. A. Munkman & Son advert

Hutsons sold kitchenware, ironmongery, lawnmowers, garden tools, mantelpieces, bedsteads, baths, gas brackets, radiators. They installed the heating system in Fishtoft Parish Church, Boston's Memorial Hall, and many others.

During the Second World War, the flat above the shop was requisitioned by the Army and used as an Officers' Mess, possibly by the 6th Battalion of the Queens Regiment which provided local defence after Dunkirk. Hand grenades and live ammunition were found on the premises for years afterwards.

A real family business, with Henry's three sons, Geoff, Bert, and Maurice coming together after the war to run the ironmongery and plumbing business, and continued by the next generation in Richard, James and John Allen. Today, it is the fourth generation in Richard's sons Douglas (Doug), and Alexander (Alex).

During archaeological work in the 1970's, the remains of an Elizabethan garden were found at the rear of the premises.

This family business continued trading until 1995, when the property was sold to be included in the Pescod Square Shopping Development. The business relocated to 65 Wide Bargate, where it still thrives.

Henry's grandson, Richard and his wife Hilary were able to purchase Simons disused builders yard at 65 Wide Bargate. The "Ironmongers" was dropped from the company name, as it no longer represented the main trading activity which was then sign making, and the well-known specialist cookshop.

Just like some other shops in town, 11, Wide Bargate will perhaps be referred to by local people for many years ahead by the name of the local family business, long after they have vacated. In this instance, it will be "Hutsons".

9 Wide Bargate

Specsavers

Relocated from 29, Market Place, this is part of a partnership of nearly 2,000 locally run businesses offering affordable optical and hearing care.

Until recently the premises was Ryman's, national stationery, art, craft and office supplies owned by Theo Paphitis, the famous entrepreneur who features in the TV series "Dragon's Den". Opened in 2008 Ryman's closed in January 2015.

Theo Paphitis was born in Cyprus, and his first business venture, at the age of 15, was to run the Tuck Shop in his school in north London.

Since then he has bought and revived Millwall FC, La Senza, Contessa Lingerie, and Stationery Box. Apart from Ryman, Boux Avenue and Robert Dyas, he has 349 stores in the UK, employs 3600 people and serves 28 million customers every year.

Another long-standing and respected local family business was here from the 1930's until recently. George R. Addy started his photographic business at No.2, Market Place (now 3 Store Mobile Phone Shop), then moved to larger premises. He was succeeded by his son Derek Addy, who together with Sydney Phillipson, became the town's leading photographers, also taking photographs for the Lincolnshire Standard.

Part of this building dates back to the mid-16th century. The site was part of a charitable bequest of Mrs. Anne Carr in 1594 and was owned by the Corporation and Charity Trustees till 1920. During renovations by Derek Addy a mid-16th Century fireplace was uncovered, together with old oak wall panelling, which today has to be maintained as part of a Listed building.

The former Ryman Stationers and JJB Sports

Occupiers since 1822 have been John Brumby, cooper; Susan Hockley and her daughters, baby linen; Robert & Charles Walker, both tailors until 1930.

Robert Walker, merchant tailor advert

5/7 Wide Bargate - Clinton Cards

5/7 Wide Bargate

Clinton Cards

This national greetings card company opened in 2014. Previous occupiers have included JJB Sports; sportswear and equipment retail. Closed in 2012 and went into administration, the business being transferred to Sports Direct, Horncastle Road.
From the 1930s this was another local family business, J. Morley and Son, sports outfitters and tobacconists. F A Morley (Albert) started the business and was succeeded by his son Roger Morley, who ran the business and also had a shop, Intersport, at 34 Market Place.
From 1860 this was occupied by Luigi Cello, born in Italy, and one of Boston's first photographers. He was succeeded by Edward Peakom in 1905, and Fred Addy in by 1913, before Addy's moved to No. 9 Wide Bargate years later.

1 and 3 Wide Bargate

Santander Bank

A Spanish, owned International Bank, Santander which acquired the Alliance and Leicester Building Society in October 2010.

Coney's Outfitters were here in the 1930s to 1950s before moving to the corner of Wide Bargate and Tawney Street. They were followed by Leicester Permanent Building Society.
The first floor is now flats, but was previously J. S. Donaldson; Sherwin and Partners, chartered architects; County Court offices.

1 and 3 Wide Bargate - Santander Bank

27 Strait Bargate

W H Smith Retail Ltd.

National Stationery, Newsagents, books, etc.

In 2014, the Post Office decided to close down their imposing and iconic premises at the entrance to Central Park, and much against the opinions of many Boston people moved the Post Office operations into the rear of W. H. Smith's shop.

To older generations of Bostonians, this will always be referred to as Wings.

In the late 19th century it was Wing and Broughton, Printers. Broughton separated and went to 42 Market place, leaving Wing & Co. Ltd. stationers and printers, with a print workshop in Mitre Lane at the rear.

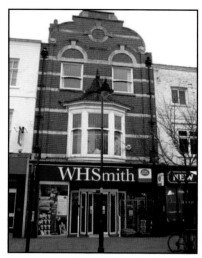

27 Strait Bargate - W H Smith

Bargate Drug Stores

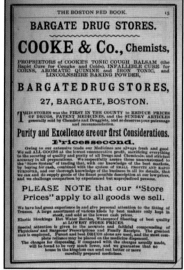

Cooke & Co. Advert

This site was occupied from 1891 to 1916 by Charles Fowler Cooke, chemist and druggist. During his time the building was destroyed by a fire on 9th September, 1905, when a young girl died, and the present building was erected

For most of the 20th century, this was Wing & Co. Ltd. Stationers and Printers, who were the foremost printers in Boston, until selling to W H Smith and Sons, Stationers in about 1963.

25 Strait Bargate - New Horizon Amusement Arcade

25 Strait Bargate

New Horizon Amusement Arcade

This family business also has premises also at Skegness, Spalding and Peterborough.

From about 1829 to 1854 this was the Post Office with Sarah Creasey as Postmistress, as well as a boot and shoe maker. She was succeeded by her son, Robert, and when he went to America the Post Office was transferred to Market Place, with the boot and shoe business being continued by others until 1905.

Later occupiers include Cowan's Fabrics, established by Harry Cowan, who also worked for Holland County Council at County Hall, Boston. He was succeeded by his son Philip Cowan, who now has a national business supplying fabrics, wallpapers, and furnishings, specialising in the hotel trade, who followed J. P. Davis (John Paxton), jeweller, watch and clockmaker; Joys Ltd., gowns and ladies dress shop.

23 Strait Bargate

There have been some recent short term lettings, including Labels 4 Less, but currently a vacant shop unit. Earlier occupiers have been Game, retail computer games, hard and software, who moved to 45 Wide Bargate.

It was a private house until 1871 when it became Charles Pickering, Hairdresser, then J. W. Burley, Greengrocer; J. Hepworth and Son Ltd. Clothiers; Leicester Building Society, which closed when merged with Alliance Building Society to become Alliance and Leicester, then taken over by Santander Bank.

23 Strait Bargate

Here is Mitre Lane, which leads to Pescod Square

21 Strait Bargate - Card Factory

21 Strait Bargate

Card Factory

National greetings card retailer.

UK's leading specialist retailer of greeting cards and associated gift and party products, its first store opened at Wakefield in 1997, and has now expanded to some 700 shops with over 6500 employees.

Modern day occupiers have been YMCA charity shop; Tchibo catalogue showroom; Thomas Cook travel agents; Montague Burton, Burtons the Tailors of Leeds.

In the 1930s the occupier was Hipps Ltd., clothiers, becoming Hepworths, later being taken over by Burtons.

Separate tenants of the first floor, with access from Mitre Lane, have included Griffiths stationers and office supplies of Sea Lane Butterwick, and Lotinga / Oasis hair salon, before they moving to Spilsby Road, near Bargate Bridge.

From 1805 it was a grocery and bakery owned by John Skinner; then Pack and Linton, drapers; then a grocery again, and in 1872 was combined with James Thorn and Co.'s drapery business at No. 19. Thorn's traded for many years until selling in 1901 to Messrs. Lacey and Garratt, who had similar businesses in Louth and Grantham as drapers, milliners and house furnishers

In the post war period this was Woolworths, before they moved across the road into the redeveloped Red Lion Hotel site.

19 Strait Bargate

Tresspass

From July 2013, this has been an outdoor clothing, camping and trekking gear, ski wear shop.

Previous occupiers during the 20th century have included Lacey & Garrett; The Bargate Stores; F W Woolworth & Co Ltd., Bazaar; Henry Field, ladies' fashions; Burtons the tailors.

19 Strait Bargate - Trespass

The Barditch

Medieval Boston was surrounded by a ditch called the "Barditch". Bar is the old word for boundary gate entrance. Just to make life complicated the street name "gate" as in "Bargate" is derived from the old Danish for street "gata".

This was a medieval semi-circular drain, probably built before 1200 as a fortification not long after the town was created, and which runs along the eastern boundary of the original Boston, parallel to the River Witham, under No. 13 Strait Bargate / under Vision Express and into Red Lion Street / New Street under Oldrids old furniture shop.

The Barditch was marked on Hall's Map of Boston, 1741, and on OS Map of 1887.

This open ditch, used as an open sewer and rubbish tip ebbing and flowing with the tide to keep it clean was later culverted, probably around the 17th century. It enters the river at the extremity of South End, opposite the end of Skirbeck Road, then runs northwards, east of the River Witham (Haven) at the rear of South End behind the Mart Yard (Boston Grammar School Courtyard), then continuing behind the Market Place, running just west of Pump Square, crossing Petticoat Lane (see the manhole circular cover in the footpath) under the centre of Oldrids, across Strait Bargate, along the rear wall of Oldrids former furniture store (now John's Furniture) and north-west into Red Lion Street to the outfall opposite the end of Union Place, near Charles Isaac's house in Witham Place.

11-17 Strait Bargate - Oldrids & Co. Ltd.

11-17 Strait Bargate

Oldrids & Co Ltd.

This is a family business established in 1804 by the first John Oldrid, and now owned and controlled by the Isaac family.

It is Boston's only department store, and is situated in the prime frontage on the walkway between the former Cattle Market and the Market Place.

The first John Oldrid founded the business of linen and woollen drapers at 11, Strait Bargate and moved his family home and business of general dealer from Hagworthingham, near Spilsby. Over the following years he purchased adjoining properties and enlarged the store. After living over the shop he bought 5 South Square, Boston in 1833 which became the family home, and is now the Co-Op Funeral Directors premises adjacent to John Adams Way at Haven Bridge, having previously been the offices of Lucas & Sharpe, chartered accountants.

John Oldrid the second lived at No. 20, Wide Bargate (now Prezzo), and it had grounds of some 20 acres, which is now Central Park, and included what is now Thorold Street, Tawney Street and the Wide Bargate frontage.

The family home of John Oldrid the third, was at 50, Wide Bargate, now the Georgians Nursing Home, but he moved into 20, Wide Bargate after the death of his grandfather.

C. M. Johnson started as an errand boy with Oldrids in 1871, and transferred to the wholesale department in 1874. By 1881, aged 24, he became a traveller, visiting the village shops which Oldrids supplied. Later still he was made manager of the wholesale department and continued until after the death of John Oldrid third's widow in 1905. When the Oldrid business was sold to a Mr. Sydney Smith, of Beverley, Yorkshire, he left and set up his own wholesale business in Red Lion Street. But Oldrids retained ownership of the premises. Eventually, after his death, that business was put up for sale by auction, and bought by Oldrids in 1951.

In 1915, Mr. Smith sold the business to Mr. Robert Isaac from Kidderminster for £10,000, and in 1918 Robert Isaac purchased the freehold property from the Oldrid family trust, followed by the rebuilding of the premises in 1919 by Boston builder, Fred Peck.

Robert Isaac interestingly, only came to Boston because of an oversight in the fine print of a business partnership.

He was a member of a prosperous West Country family of farmers, but he became a partner in a department store in Kidderminster. He was also a man of action (an instinct not foreign in the Isaac family of Boston). He was in partnership in a drapery business with a farmer. Eventually Robert felt that his partner was more concerned with his farming than the drapery business so suggested that the partnership be dissolved. He thought his partner would jump at the idea of Robert buying him out. However the fine print of the partnership agreement stated that the partner who wished to dissolve the partnership must give the other partner first refusal. So Robert had to sell to his partner. He was now without a business, he looked around for one, and found it in Boston. And as they say, the rest is history.

Robert had five children, three sons, William Augustus (Gus), Robert Stuart and Charles Kenneth, and two daughters, Florence Stella and Hester Mary.

Two sons, Gus and Ken eventually assisted in running the business. Gus went off to war, after cutting his apprenticeship short in Worcester and he persuaded Robert to buy a business in Chippenham in 1924, which he ran successfully for several years. He returned to Boston in 1931 and re-joined his brother Ken in the business - which allowed their father to retire from Oldrids.
Robert Isaac was a keen golfer and a promoter of the game in Boston.

On retiring from the business, he handed over control to his sons Gus and Ken, with Gus being the senior director.

Gus married Jessie Beaulah, a member of the well- known Beaulah family who owned J & J Beaulah, canners and wholesale Distributors in 1923.

They had six children, Anthea Doreen, Robert Beaulah (Bob), Augustus William (Bill), John Beaulah, David Ward, Adrian Bennett.

Mr. Gus, as he was known to all employees, had a strict rule that all the boys had training and experience outside Oldrids and Boston before taking up employment in the family business. The one exception was David, who joined his uncle Gerald Beaulah in wholesale distributors G N Beaulah Ltd. in Pump Square, and later in Tattershall Road.

During Mr. Gus' period as Oldrids managing director, Oldrids acquired the wholesale drapery business of C M Johnson and Son which was then formed into a limited company. As the younger generation of the family came into the business, Oldrids grew steadily and expanded by introducing sales of furniture, sports, prams, books and the present department store with restaurant, hairdressing, beauty salon, was also taking shape

When Mr. Gus fully retired in 1968, his eldest son Robert Beaulah Isaac took over as managing director, and the youngest son Adrian became general manager responsible for staff engagement and training plus the day to day running of the business. During Bob's tenure Oldrids grew rapidly with the developments of Oldrids Downtown in Boston and Grantham, and the Oldrids idea of the Pescod Square development began to take shape.

When Mr. Bob retired in 1987, the baton was passed to Adrian Bennett Isaac, the youngest of Mr. Gus' five sons. Mr. Adrian ('Mr. Energy' himself wouldn't walk when he could run, and even when climbing staircases he would take two steps at a time).

Adrian Isaac

For Mr. Adrian his work rate made everyday appear to have 36 hours in it.

He was the ideal person to make the Pescod Square dream a reality and when the Boston Chamber of Commerce came up with the idea of security cameras being installed in the town centre, the task of raising the initial money was given to him. He was at that time a very energetic Chairman of the Chamber's Retail Division.

His immediate response was the usual *"It's going to be difficult getting money out of retailers, so let's get on with it."* He asked, begged, cajoled and bullied, got the money and had the first set of security cameras installed.

Mr. Adrian retired in 2002, and the baton of leadership was passed on to his nephew Martin Isaac, the son of David Ward Isaac. At the time he was managing Grantham Downtown. He inherited the task of seeing Pescod Square development take off and guiding Oldrids main store to compete with national companies then arriving in Boston.

In 2012, he joined forces with his cousin Robert Isaac in a furniture business in Newark.

Mr. Adrian returned as head of Oldrids for a short period until a new Chief Executive was appointed. Martin was following a new trend in the Oldrid/Isaac saga.

The family made a break with tradition and went in search of a non-Isaac, non-family CEO, and in doing so appointed Ms. Ann Marie McClintock as its new head. She came with a career in Department Stores, and it is fair to say that the impact in store was indeed noticeable, and desirable, and yet the talk around town was that Oldrids had something missing, maybe because there were no Isaac men around. The humanity in the store had gone. Alas, Ms. McClintock has left to pursue other interests. In my opinion, for what it's worth she has left a fine store of which the Isaac family and the town of Boston can be justly proud.

My latest information is that Martin has temporarily taken on the role of non-Executive Chairman, whilst a new CEO is found.

There have also been two major additions to the Oldrids operation. The company has leased a town centre store in Gainsborough (as Oldrids), and an edge of city store from the Lincolnshire Co-Op Society in Lincoln trading as Downtown.

Bob Isaac's son, David, joined with his cousin, Chris Isaac, in taking over the "Sack Store" in one of the old railway goods agents warehouses at Redstone Industrial Estate, Spalding Road, Boston. That partnership broke up, and David joined forces with his father's cousin, Garth Isaac, father Bob, and mother Margaret in purchasing Johnsons Garden Centre on the Wainfleet Road in Boston.

Cousins, Bob and Garth, together with Oldrids company secretary, Mr. John Ball and his wife purchased premises in Wide Bargate, Boston and converted them into the Georgians Nursing Home.

Robert Isaac had two other sons, Stuart and Charles Kenneth popularly known by the Boston public as Ken Isaac, and by his employees as Mr. Ken. Stuart moved away, and Ken stayed in Boston with his brother Gus to develop Oldrids. His forte was lino, carpets, etc. Ken was a strong man, an athlete, strong swimmer, boatman, and was said a bit eccentric. During the Second World War, he served locally in the Observer Corps.

Mr. Ken married Jessie Alvena Armes in 1933, and had seven children - Alvena Ann; Charles Stuart; Robin Augustus; Dorothy Stella Jane; Primrose Jill; Edgar Hedley Garth and Ernest Norman Rodney.

The four boys (just as in the case of Gus' sons) received their retail training and business experience away from Boston and Oldrids.

Garth and Charles focussed on furniture, Robin on carpets and Rodney on sales and marketing. Rodney was quite prominent in the Chamber of Commerce in the early 1990s. He worked tirelessly in promoting tourism, especially between Boston and Polish towns. Boston unfortunately lost a good ambassador due to his untimely death at the age of just 49, in 1992.

This is just a glimpse of the Oldrids/Isaac Saga, a scan through the eyes of a Jamaican immigrant who 65 years ago had the good fortune to be interviewed by Mr. Gerald Beaulah and Mr. Gus Isaac for a job as bookkeeper/cashier at G N Beaulah, then in Pump Square, and given the job on the spot, having been advised by the local labour Exchange that he would never get such a job In Boston.

If you want a real insight into this family business saga, get hold of a copy of "Oldrids of Boston Story" by Adrian Isaac. It is available in Oldrids main store book department in Strait Bargate, where the business has been located for 211 years.

Mr. Gus always said the reasons for Oldrid's existence to give a service to the people of Boston, to improve the wellbeing of the employees, and to provide work for the many male Isaacs.

In the 1920s Ken Isaac dived into the river Witham from the Town Bridge and swam up to the Sluice Bridge.

1924 saw Robert and Gus purchase Mr. Hiscox's shop in Chippenham, which they subsequently sold in 1931 when Gus returned to Boston.

In 1951 Bob came into the business as company secretary; Adrian was relief errand boy during the holidays in the 1950's and returned to Boston, becoming general manager in 1968.

Like all his brothers, Adrian was educated at Bootham Quaker Boarding School in York, where he ran a "pawn shop in the school". In the holidays he was relief errand boy in the 1950s.

In 1959 he joined Griffin and Spalding's store, owned by Debenhams, as a junior sales before being called home in 1961 as Gus couldn't find anyone to be the buyer for men's and boy's.

In 1968 Adrian Isaac took over from Gus Isaac as staff engager and general manager. Then in 1987, Adrian took over from Bob as managing director, on Bob's retirement.

1973 saw Oldrid's purchase a five acre site at Wyberton Chain Bridge, from Jack Mountain, the Boston family pork butcher, which was developed into what is now Oldrid's Downtown. In 1981, and for some four years, this included a Peugeot main agency garage.

This was followed in 1987 with the development of a 10 acre site at Grantham, just off the A1. This 103,000 square feet store which subsequently incorporated the Boundary Mill fashion store.

Today, and for the time being, there is no chief executive, and the business is conducted by the accountant, general manager, and personnel manager, with Martin Isaac as non-executive chairman.

Previous occupiers of parts of these Strait Bargate premises have included Dr. Patrick Francis, who had George Bass, the world famous surgeon and explorer of Australia, as an apprentice. George Bass was born in Aswarby, Sleaford, educated at Boston Grammar School under Rev. Obadiah Bell, and qualified to the Company of Surgeons in 1794, before joining the Royal Navy as a naval surgeon. His world wide fame came when he sailed with Matthew Flinders who circumnavigated what was then Van Diemen's Land and is now Australia. The passage between there and the mainland was named, Bass Strait in his honour.

No. 13, directly over the Barditch, (and now in the middle of Oldrids frontage), was a printing works, firstly Robert Roberts, who first printed the Boston Guardian in 1854. Robinson Stubley succeeded Roberts, and then it became Arthur Broughton and Frederick Wing. Broughton moved to Market Place, and Wing stayed here until 1920.

9 Strait Bargate

Cooplands Bakery

This family business of bakers and confectioners opened in Boston in August 2012.

Cooplands and Son (Scarborough) Ltd. was founded in 1885 as a pork butcher and bakery in Market Street, Scarborough by the present managing director's great grandfather. Now with the fourth generation of the family involved, the business has become one of the country's leading craft bakers with 1,000 employees, 100 shops and 10 cafes in Yorkshire, Durham, Lincolnshire and Teesside.

9 Strait Bargate - Cooplands Bakery

Previous modern day occupiers have been Thomas Cook, travel agents who relocated to Pescod Square; Air Tours; Radio Rentals (1970s).

In the first half of the 20th century premises were occupied by the local business of Bailey and Alexander, Chemists, having succeeded S. Pilley, chemist, whose family business had been here from 1841. The present day opticians' practice Peebles and Hilton, now located in Tawney Street was born in 1954, when David Peebles came to work for Will Alexander. He operated an optician's practice from the first floor front room, with the bay window looking out on to Strait Bargate and Mason's shoe shop.

7 Strait Bargate - EE

7 Strait Bargate

EE

National mobile phone network company, formerly T-Mobile.

Earlier tenants were birthdays, national company and part of Clinton Cards Group, greeting cards and gifts. Lennard's Ltd., shoe shop followed by Manfield Footwear. In the early 1900s it was Sterlings Ltd., Bootmakers, and Scales and Son Ltd., boot manufacturers.

5 Strait Bargate

Phones 4 U

This shop closed in September 2014, going into administration with Price Waterhouse Cooper. Loans and debts amounted to £258 million.

Previous occupiers from 1893 have included Parker & Smith, drapers and silk merchants; Arthur Harrison, draper, costumier and milliner from about 1896, successor to Parker and Smith; Wyles Bros.; A. Richardson; Stephenson, Smart and Co.; Herbert E. Richardson, Outfitter; Brown Brothers and Taylor Ltd., furnishers; Dale Forty and Co. Ltd., radio and television dealers; Wigfalls; Rumbelows, radio TV and electricals; Radio Rentals.

It became Westminster Bank. When Westminster Bank merged with National Provincial Bank in 1970, it closed.
Note the typical 1960s design of the false roof line, which still exists.

5 Strait Bargate - Phones 4 U

3 Strait Bargate - Vodaphone Ltd

3 Strait Bargate

Vodaphone Ltd

National Mobile Phone Shop.

In the late 18th century, the main draper in Boston was West Wheldale at Nos. 1,3,and 5 Strait Bargate. They downsized into No. 5, but John Wheldale carried on at No. 3 till 1854. He was followed by Smith, Draper, then Robinson and Smith, Grocers moved in until 1880, it became Tom Kitwood, Wine and Spirits & Grocery.

The Patent Still Pub, recorded in 1896 as being owned by Thomas and Tom Kitwood (formerly Robinson and Smith), then remaining in the Kitwood family becoming T.Kitwood & Sons, Wholesale grocers (In 1931 Alderman Thomas Kitwood was given the Freedom of the Borough). The Kitwood's manager was George Harwood.
The pub was also known as Garden of Eden.

There was a private bar upstairs which was only available to invited guests. There was no barman on duty to serve you, and all gentlemen were on their honour to place a £1 note in the large ashtray on the bar whenever they bought a drink or a round of drinks.

The property was sold to Oldrids in 1967 for £40,000, and rebuilt to become their pram and toy shop, having incorporated Bests Silver Cross Prams in West Street; then Oldrids fashions and menswear.

This property was then sold and it became Greenwoods Menswear, which eventually moved in 2008 to 48 Market Place, before closing in Boston in 2014.

The first floor above Greenwoods was Russell, Son and Scanlon (later Weller, Russell and Laws), insurance brokers. It's Principal was Charles Russell, who then moved to Red Lion Street, being replaced by the Boston Target, who in turn moved to 16 Wide Bargate.

T. Kitwood & Sons advert

1 Strait Bargate and 1 Market Place

F Hinds Ltd, National Jewellery Chain Shop.

This is recorded in the book Memories of Boston Market Place, 1949-2009.

1 Strait Bargate & 1 Market Place - F Hinds Ltd

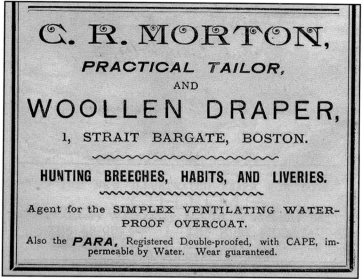

C. R. Morton advert

In 1822 the premises were occupied by John Morton, printer and bookseller. After rebuilding in 1866, it was later leased to Harold H. Dodds who continued as a printer and bookseller until his death in 1915.

Additional occupiers have included C. R. Morton, tailor and outfitter (1893); Cherry Corner Café; Freeman Hardy and Willis, footwear; Michelle's dress shop (1950s-60s) owned by Rene Ashton/O'Shaughnessy, moving to Exchange Buildings in the Market Place.

Books written by author Ralph Ottey

Little London, Jamaica and me 1924-1944

Stranger Bwoy in ihe Royal Air Force in Lincolnshire 1944-148

You'll never get a job here in Boston 1949-1989

Tales of Old St. Paul's

A short history of Little London, Jamaica 1924 1948

Tales of Old St. Paul's - volume 2

Colourful recipes from old Jamaica

Memories of Boston Market Place 1949-2009

Memories of Bargate in Boston, Lincolnshire published August 2015

Reader's Notes

David Carr

Peter Lawson

A young Dudley Bryant on a bad day on the market

Mrs Julie Hallgate and staff

Phil Harris

John Lingard

Garth Isaac

Tony Cammack

June and Gladys Holmes

Doug, Richard and Alex

Jim Mather